The Public and
The National Agenda

How People Learn About Important Issues

The Public and The National Agenda

How People Learn About Important Issues

Wayne Wanta
University of Oregon

LAWRENCE ERLBAUM ASSOCIATES, PUBLISHERS
1997 Mahwah, New Jersey **London**

Lawrence Erlbaum Associates, Inc., Publishers
10 Industrial Avenue
Mahwah, New Jersey 07430

Library of Congress Cataloging-in-Publication-Data
    Wanta, Wayne.
The public and the national agenda: how people learn about
important issues / by Wayne Wanta/
      p. cm.
    Includes bibliographic references and index.
    ISBN 0-8058-2460-X (cloth : alk. paper).
    ISBN 0-8058-2461-8 (pbk. : alk. paper)
1. Mass media—Political aspects. 2. Press and politics. 3.
Mass media—Audiences. 4. Mass media and public
opinion. I. Title.
    P95.8.W36   1997
    302.23—dc21

                       97-3347
                       CIP

Books published by Lawrence Erlbaum Associates are printed
on acid-free paper, and their bindings are chosen for strength
and durability.

Printed in the United States of America
10 9 8 7 6 5 4 3 2 1

CONTENTS

Preface   vii

1 Theoretical Underpinnings of the Agenda-   1
   Setting Process

2 The Agenda-Setting Susceptibility Measure   5

3 Effects of Demographic and Psychological   20
   Variables on Agenda Setting

4 Effects of Behavioral Variables on Agenda   36
   Setting

5 Putting It All Together: How the   48
   Agenda-Setting Process Works

6 Effects of Different Media on Agenda Setting   62

7 The Role of Nonmedia Sources in the Agenda-   79
   Setting Process

8 Expanding the Agenda-Setting Hypothesis   92

9 Social Learning in the Agenda-Setting Process   101

References   111

Author Index   117

Subject Index   121

Preface

More than a decade ago (actually, the year was 1985), I was first introduced to the concept of *agenda setting* in a graduate-level mass communication theory course taught by Professor James Tankard, Jr. at the University of Texas. It was here that I first heard the hypothesis that, through their coverage of issues, mass media give the public salience cues regarding the relative importance of these issues.

My initial reaction was: No kidding. As a former newspaper copy editor and page designer, I was often in charge of deciding which issues were deserving of prominent display and which issues were to be ignored. It was our job as journalists to tell the public what was important. We had a different term than *agenda setting* for this notion, however. We called it *news judgment*. Nonetheless, I found the concept of agenda setting intriguing, logical and important.

To my good fortune, Maxwell McCombs joined the University of Texas faculty less than a year later. Under his mentoring, I learned that agenda setting was a much more complex process than a simple, linear relationship between an information producer and an information consumer.

The years have passed, and the learning process continues. This book is the culmination of my research up to the present. It details several studies that attempted to examine agenda setting from the news consumers' standpoint.

The following pages detail what I think is very practical research. Indeed, agenda setting has always been a very practical area of research to me, ever since my first reaction linking it to journalistic news judgment.

In general, the research here supports the notion that individuals are active processors of mass media messages, a conclusion that will be repeated throughout the book. Again, this conclusion seems very logical and practical. Individuals decide how and why they use the news media. Thus, individuals determine, to a large degree, the magnitude of agenda-setting effects that they will display based on their backgrounds, attitudes, and actions.

The research here, then, combines agenda setting with uses and gratifications research. These two areas form a natural link. This book looks at the mental processing of issue salience cues at several stages. The first two chapters form the theoretical background for the agenda-setting projects from which the data were gathered. Chapter 1 provides a look at the historical circumstances from which agenda setting emerged. Chapter 2 details the methodology employed, including an explanation of the survey sites and the agenda-setting susceptibility measure that forms the basis of the subsequent analyses.

The next three chapters examine individual-level variables and their role in the agenda-setting process. Chapter 3 examines the influence of demographics and psychological variables on agenda setting. Chapter 4 investigates behavioral variables and agenda setting. Chapter 5 ties the previous two chapters together and proposes and tests a causal model of agenda setting.

The next two chapters examine factors outside the individual that may influence the agenda-setting process. Chapter 6 looks at differences between print and broadcast media in agenda setting. Chapter 7 examines the role that important public officials, such as the president of the United States, play in agenda setting.

Chapter 8 discusses a new direction in agenda-setting research, namely the influence of media exposure on the diversity of issues with which individuals are concerned. Chapter 9 provides concluding remarks and discusses the implications of the results.

This book could not have been possible without the help of several individuals. I list some of them here, knowing full well that I am apt to forget some key figures.

I must start with Max McCombs. Max has been not only a mentor, but a great friend as well. I owe my success in the mass communication research field to Max. He has been my role model. I wish all beginning scholars could have as wonderful of a relationship with their mentors as I have had with Max.

I also must thank my other mentors at the University of Texas, especially Jim Tankard, who provided great insights on both my thesis and dissertation; Wayne Danielson, who mentored me in the quantitative research methods that I now embrace; Pam Shoemaker, who took a confused graduate student and steered him in the right direction; and Gene Burd, who helped me look at mass communication research in unusual, but important ways.

I thank my former colleagues at Southern Illinois University at Carbondale, especially William Elliott, now the dean at Marquette; Walter Jaehnig, Erwin Atwood, and Joe Foote, the current SIU dean. They gave me the support and friendship I needed to launch my career.

I thank my current colleagues at Oregon, especially Jim Lemert, Arnold Ismach, and Duncan McDonald. They have helped me flourish while living in the paradise that is Oregon.

I thank my colleagues and coauthors through the years, especially Randy Miller of South Florida, the best friend a person could ask for; Thomas Johnson of SIU, whose warped sense of humor is surpassed only by my own.

Of course, I must thank all of my former students who have contributed in various ways to my career, especially Joseph and Debbie Hu and Tsien-tsung Lee. They keep me thinking. Without them, life would be awfully dull.   —Wayne Wanta

1

Theoretical Underpinnings of the Agenda-Setting Process

On the surface, the agenda-setting hypothesis appears to be very simple. News media coverage gives salience cues to the members of the public, showing them which issues are important. The public receives these salience cues and ultimately believes that the issues receiving extensive coverage are more important than those issues receiving little coverage.

However, the concept of *agenda setting* is much more complex. Not all people demonstrate identical agenda-setting effects. Not all issues influence individuals equally. Not all types of coverage influence individuals in the same manner. An endless list of factors intervene in this process.

Regardless, the agenda-setting hypothesis has been widely supported under a variety of conditions. More than two decades since the initial study examining this press–public interface was published (McCombs & Shaw, 1972), agenda setting remains an important area of mass communication research. It has certainly withstood the test of time and replication.

There have been refinements, indeed. Yet, the agenda-setting hypothesis has retained its basic premise that the news media's coverage of issues influences the public's perceived importance of issues.

Of concern in this book is how the agenda-setting process functions within individuals. The data examined differ from the vast majority of agenda-setting research in two significant ways.

First, the analysis here uses the individual, and not the issue, as the unit of measurement. Because the data focus on the individual, they offer several insights into the information processing involved in agenda setting. Although agenda setting at its broadest sense is a societal effect —influencing a mass public — it nonetheless begins within individuals. Individuals consume media coverage; individuals process this coverage; and individuals learn from this coverage. The social learning of important issues is the basis of agenda setting.

Second, the analysis examines an *agenda-setting susceptibility measure* rather than one response to one open-ended question. As seen later, the agenda-setting susceptibility measure is actually an index comprised of several items that more accurately demonstrate the magnitude of agenda-setting effects that individuals display. Rather than base the magnitude of agenda-setting effects on one survey response, as the traditional agenda-setting question ("What is the number one problem facing our country?") does, the agenda-setting susceptibility measure, by tracking how concerned individuals are with several highly covered issues, is a more sensitive measure of this mass media effect.

ISSUE SALIENCE

Weaver (1984) noted that two major assumptions drive agenda-setting research. First, the news media do not mirror reality, but instead filter and shape it. Journalists, in other words, choose what issues and events they will cover and how they will cover them. Second, emphasis by the media, over time on a relatively small number of issues, leads the public into perceiving these issues as more important than other issues. The more an issue gets covered, the more it will be perceived as being important by members of the public. It is this second assumption that is the basis for the agenda-setting hypothesis.

Agenda setting, then, is a type of social learning. Individuals learn about the relative importance of issues in society through the amount of coverage the issues receive in the news media. Thus, the more coverage an issue receives, the more concern individuals have with the issue. In other words, individuals learn how concerned they should be through the amount of coverage the issue receives. Agenda-setting research, therefore, is concerned with individuals' cognitions.

Despite the extensive amount of research examining agenda setting, relatively little is known about the mental processing of information that takes place within individuals. How is issue salience transmitted from the news media to individuals? What are the stages of this message transferral? Most important, what factors affect the transferral of issue salience cues? These questions, then, are the driving force behind this text.

Cognitions—social or otherwise—can be influenced by several factors, including education level and other demographics, motivations to learn, and behavioral characteristics of individuals. Thus, some of the same variables that affect academic learning will be investigated here through the social learning function of agenda setting.

The notion that agenda setting is social learning, while appearing logical on the surface, was not the initial idea proposed in agenda-setting research. In fact, Shaw and McCombs (1977) described agenda-setting as an inadvertent byproduct of media exposure. They wrote that "Both by deliberate winnowing and by inadvertent agenda-setting the mass media help society achieve consensus on which concerns and interests should be translated into public issues and opinions" (p. 152). This suggests that agenda setting is more of an incidental learning process than an active cognitive process. In other words, people learn salience cues almost by accident through their exposure to the mass media.

Uses and gratifications researchers, however, would argue against this approach. People are problem solvers who approach situations as opportunities to gain new knowledge (see McGuire, 1974). Individuals, then, actively seek to fulfill information needs by selecting and using the news media. And so, it is clear that research is needed to clear up these discrepancies.

AGENDA SETTING THROUGH THE YEARS

Hundreds of mass communication studies have examined the concept of agenda setting since the seminal study by McCombs and Shaw (1972). McCombs (1992), in his introduction to a special section of *Journalism Quarterly* devoted to the 20th anniversary of the initial agenda-setting study, categorized all previous agenda-setting research into four phases.

Phase 1 involved initial examinations of the agenda-setting process. Studies in this category involved simple tests, comparing media coverage of issues with the public's issue concerns. Among these studies were the initial McCombs and Shaw (1972) study and the follow-up Shaw and McCombs (1977) investigation in Charlotte, North Carolina.

Phase 2 involved the exploration of the contingent conditions that enhance or inhibit agenda-setting effects. Included in this grouping were studies by Hill (1985), who examined the influence of demographics in agenda setting, and a whole series of studies that investigated interpersonal communication (Atwater, Salwen, & Anderson, 1985; Erbring, Goldenberg, & Miller, 1980; Hong & Shemer, 1976;). Indeed, agenda setting does not exist in isolation. Many factors affect the magnitude of the effect.

Phase 3 explored candidate images and political interest as alternative agendas. Weaver, Graber, McCombs, and Eyal (1981), for example, provided several insights into the role of attitudes in the processing of salience cues among voters. Thus, research in this area looked beyond the press agenda–public agenda linkage by investigating psychological factors inherent in the agenda-setting process.

Phase 4 introduced a new question into the agenda-setting arena by asking: "Who sets the press' agenda?" These studies—for example, Wanta, Stephenson, Turk, and McCombs (1989)—moved agenda setting into an earlier point in time in the public opinion process by examining potential sources of the news media agenda. Public officials are important sources for news stories. Thus, these same public officials can potentially influence the agenda of issues that the news media cover.

This book investigates all four phases of agenda-setting research. First, it examines the original agenda-setting hypothesis: News media coverage of issues will influence the perceived importance of the issues held by members of the public. The agenda-setting process, indeed, is the basis for this text.

This book also concentrates on the contingent conditions under which agenda setting takes place. It examines behavioral variables, such as level of media exposure and interpersonal communication, as well as other factors that may affect agenda setting.

In addition, the book investigates interest in politics as well as other psychological variables. Respondent attitudes should play a role in the agenda-setting process. As is discussed later, respondents' attitudes are powerful determinants of the magnitude of the agenda-setting effects that they ultimately display.

Finally, the book investigates additional sources of issue salience (i.e., the president of the United States). Respondents may pick up issue salience cues from important public officials, such as the president, as previous research suggests (see Wanta et al., 1989).

2

The Agenda-Setting
Susceptibility Measure

Researchers have operationalized the agenda-setting effect in a wide variety of ways, with varying degrees of success. This chapter outlines some of the methodological difficulties these researchers have faced and how the measure examined in subsequent chapters—the agenda-setting susceptibility index—is much more rigorous and accurate than measures previously used.

INDIVIDUALS AS THE UNIT OF MEASUREMENT

A consistent problem with many previous agenda-setting studies has been how to examine individuals as the unit of measurement. A great many previous studies have employed the issue as the unit of measurement. In other words, surveys asked respondents, "What is the number one problem facing our country today?" The responses were then aggregated across issues. Thus, the issue was the unit of measurement for all subsequent data analyses.

However, individuals, and not issues, are the focus of this book. Indeed, individuals should be the focus of more research in agenda-setting. It is the individual who consumes and processes issue information contained in the news media; it is the individual who ultimately displays the agenda-setting effect.

Although agenda setting may be a societal effect, the process of agenda-setting takes place within individuals. Several researchers previously have called for more in-depth investigations of agenda setting at the individual level of analysis. McCombs and Weaver (1985) argued that an individual analysis can investigate audience transactions with the media and factors that influence this relationship. They noted that agenda setting "can be a fruitful bridge between the effects tradition and the uses and gratification tradition" (p. 108).

Uses and gratifications research does form a natural link with agenda setting. As Blumler and Katz (1974) argued, researchers should "ask not what media do to people, but ask what people do with media." Thus, research in this area embraces a concept of an active audience. Active processing of salience cues transmitted by the media should lead to strong agenda-setting effects with individuals.

As Katz, Blumler, and Gurevitch (1974) noted, the uses and gratifications approach is concerned with: "(1) the social and psychological origins of (2) needs, which generate (3) expectations of (4) the mass media or other sources which lead to (5) differential patterns of media exposure (or engagement in other activities), resulting in (6) need gratifications and (7) other consequences, perhaps mostly unintended ones" (p. 20). Thus, the analysis on which this book is based presupposes that the consequences of an individual's exposure to the mass media—variable number seven in the Katz et al. (1974) model—is an agenda-setting effect. The other variables are stages that individuals go through before the agenda-setting effect emerges.

Agenda-setting effects, therefore, logically should be most pronounced for active participants. Active participants are more attentive to information transmitted through the media and, therefore, should more efficiently process the salience cues contained in the media messages.

CONCEPTUAL PROBLEMS WITH AGENDA SETTING

A comparison of two hypothetical media consumers might illustrate the incredibly complex process of agenda setting.

Case 1 is an unemployed construction worker. Demographically, he ranks low in education and income. He is also a low media user. When asked what he thinks is the number one problem facing our country today, he might say, "the economy," because he believes the state of the economy is the reason he is unemployed. In addition, although this individual may not be an avid newspaper reader, he may have discussed his employment problems with other unemployed persons. Thus, these interpersonal discussions may have reinforced his belief that the economy is in dire health. Moreover, he may have seen firsthand that the economy is struggling with unemployment during his last visit to the crowded unemployment office.

Case 2 is a highly successful attorney, who is also the mother of three. She ranks high in education and income, and she is a high media user. Unemployment and the economy do not directly concern her. Her job has provided financial security for her family. When asked what she thinks is the number one problem facing our country today, however, she, nonetheless, might say, "the economy," because she may have recently read several newspaper articles predicting a sharp downturn in the economy for the near future, or a few articles discussing unemployment in the construction industry. Media coverage of the economy, then, may have given her the impression that the economy is the most important problem facing our country today.

Thus, both individuals may believe that the broad category of economy is the most important problem facing our country today. They reached this opinion, however, in vastly different ways. Yet, in an agenda-setting study, employing aggregate data, these two individuals would be grouped together because of their similar response on the single most important issue question. Aggregate data would not allow for examinations of the mental processing of information or other factors that may influence the agenda-setting process.

Obviously, factors other than media coverage came into play for these two individuals. An issue-based analysis would lose sight of these factors.

The information processing in agenda setting, then, is ripe for an intensive examination. The stages leading from news production to issue salience is incredibly complex. Investigations of agenda setting at the individual level have been confounded with methodological pitfalls.

THE CONCEPT OF AGENDA SETTING

Conceptually, agenda setting involves the social learning of the relative importance of issues through the coverage that the issues receive in the news media. In short, the more coverage that an issue receives, the more members of a community perceive the issue to be important.

Agenda setting, then, takes place at an early stage of public opinion, a stage in which the public becomes aware of a potential problem. Indeed, awareness of a problem is a necessary first step before implementation of solutions to the problem can be proposed and instituted.

OPERATIONALIZING AGENDA-SETTING EFFECTS

Researchers have struggled with ways of operationalizing the end result of the agenda-setting process, namely the effect of mass media. The initial agenda-setting study of McCombs and Shaw (1972) used aggregate data and employed the issue as the unit of measurement. They found that the list of issues that their respondents felt were important closely matched the coverage these issues received in the news media, thus, supporting the agenda-setting hypothesis.

Although the studies in Chapel Hill (McCombs & Shaw, 1972) and Charlotte (Shaw & McCombs, 1977) provided important first steps in operationalizing the concept of agenda setting, several important questions about the processing of salience cues remained. Shifting the unit of measurement from the issue to the individual was necessary for an in-depth analysis of the agenda-setting process.

However, using the individual as the unit of measurement poses problems for agenda-setting researchers. The traditional agenda-setting question ("What is the number one problem facing our country today?") produces nominal data (an issue). Responses, thus, are difficult to quantify—each response is the number one problem facing our country today, regardless of what issue respondents mention. In other words, whether respondents say, "economy," "crime," or "bad weather," their response is number one. Therefore, coding their answers is methodologically difficult.

Clearly, the simplest way to transform the nominal issue responses into interval data is to group all responses into issue categories. Thus, if the mass of respondents list *crime* more often than *economy* as the number one problem facing our country today, then the issue of crime is more important than the issue of the economy for the aggregate public. This aggregate public can then be compared with the agenda of issues covered by the news media. Indeed, this is precisely the methodology employed by most early agenda-setting researchers.

Focusing on the issue rather than the individual is appropriate under certain circumstances. For example, Atwater, Salwen, and Anderson (1985) examined coverage of subissues dealing with pollution. Thus, aggregated data allowed for a rigorous examination of an issue variable.

Aggregate data also allow for broad examinations of large publics, an especially key consideration for early investigations in an area of research. Thus, by utilizing the issue as the unit of measurement, the McCombs and Shaw (1972) study was able to examine the general applicability of this broad-based societal concept.

However, using the issue as the unit of measurement poses some serious disadvantages—the largest disadvantage being that when you aggregate data, you can no longer analyze the individual. In a study using the issue as the unit of analysis, both the construction worker and the attorney mentioned earlier would be grouped together under economy. Yet, these two individuals used entirely different criteria in forming their opinion. The different criteria, however, would be lost by using only the issue as the unit of analysis.

A TYPOLOGY OF
AGENDA-SETTING METHODOLOGIES

Previous agenda-setting research can be categorized in several ways. One useful typology was introduced by McCombs (1981), who argued that all agenda-setting research can be categorized into four groups based on two factors: the type of data utilized (aggregate or individual) and the type of issue (single issue or issue sets). McCombs, Danielian, and Wanta (1995) further detailed the resulting categories and labeled them mass persuasion, automaton, natural history, and cognitive portrait. The typology is shown in Fig. 2.1. The four categories are briefly discussed here.

Mass Persuasion Studies. These studies focus on sets of issues and on aggregated data. These studies mainly view agenda setting from the societal level—respondents as a group. This was the typology for many of the early studies in agenda setting, including the initial McCombs and Shaw (1972) study and the early research of Funkhouser (1973).

Weaver (1994) pointed out an important distinction about mass persuasion studies. These studies do not show that the news media influenced individuals' agendas, but instead demonstrate that the media influence the *distribution* of the top one or two issues among some population. As Weaver noted:

> Even though this is not as dramatic an effect as some advocates of agenda-setting might hope for, it is still an important phenomenon, for it suggests that the relative amount of emphasis on various issues by the media determines the size of various groups of individuals in a given community or society who are most concerned about these same issues. (p. 683)

Mass persuasion studies have employed a very simple operationalization of the agenda-setting effect.

Measurement of the agenda

		Aggregate data	Individual data
	Set of issues	Mass Persuasion	Automaton
Focus of attention	Single issue	Natural History	Cognitive Portrait

FIG. 2.1. Agenda-setting typology. From "Issues in the News and Public Agenda: The Agenda Setting Tradition," by Mc Combs, Danielian, & Wanta, 1995. In Public Opinion and the Communication of Consent (p. 285), by T. L. Glasser & C. T. Salmon (Eds.), 1995, New York: Guilford Press. Copyright © 1995 by Guilford Press. Reprinted with permission.

McCombs and Shaw (1972), for example, used a cross-sectional survey in Chapel Hill, North Carolina, asking respondents what they thought were the key issues of the 1968 presidential campaign. The issues were rank-ordered based on the percentage of respondents who named the issues as important. This public agenda was then compared with content from television, newspapers, and news magazines. They found a strong correlation between the two issue agendas ($r = .967; p < .001$).

Funkhouser (1973) compared data from the Gallup polls that asked, "What is the number one problem facing our country today?" with media coverage in three weekly magazines—*Time*, *Newsweek*, and *U.S. News*. The number of articles dealing with issues mentioned in all Gallup polls from 1960 to 1970 were highly correlated with Gallup responses to the most important problem question ($r = .78; p < .001$). Thus, the amount of coverage issues received in the decade of the 1960s closely matched the issue concerns reported in Gallup polls for the same time period.

Automaton Studies.   These studies examine sets of issues and individual agendas. Very few agenda-setting studies can be classified here. Indeed, McCombs et al. (1995) noted that there would be little reason to expect an individual to perfectly mirror the ranking of issues covered in the news media. A study by McLeod, Becker, and Byrnes (1974) is perhaps the purest example of automaton studies. In their study, they found only limited support for the agenda-setting hypothesis when they asked individuals to rank-order six or more issues.

A closer look at McLeod et al.'s (1974) operationalization of agenda setting gives some indication of why few researchers have either attempted studies that would fit into this category of methodology or have found support for the agenda-setting hypothesis. McLeod et al. asked potential voters to rank six issues on their level of relative importance. These rankings were then compared with the coverage these issues received in two competing newspapers.

Issue agendas for the two newspapers varied greatly. In addition, the authors found only some support for the agenda-setting hypothesis. This limited support, however, could be attributed to one specific issue. Here, the media gave a great deal of coverage to honesty in government, but the public rated it average. Thus, although many issue ranks were relatively consistent across the public and press agendas, one of the six issues—honesty in government—may have minimized the observed agenda-setting effect found here.

Relatively few automaton studies have been undertaken in agenda setting. Moreover, Weaver (1994) concluded that studies of this type, which typically compare the ranking of a set of issues emphasized by the media with the ranking of those same issues by individuals, generally do not offer much support for the agenda-setting hypothesis. As Weaver noted: "This is not terribly surprising, given the stringency of the test (media ranking of a set of issues transferred intact to each individual in the study)" (p. 687).

Natural History Studies.   These studies examine agenda-setting effects across single issues with aggregate public agenda data.

Several studies in this classification have found powerful agenda-setting effects. Winter and Eyal (1981), for example, found an agenda-setting influence of the news media for the civil rights issue. Other research in this area includes Lang and Lang (1983) and MacKuen and Coombs (1981).

Winter and Eyal (1981) operationalized the agenda-setting effect by tracking one issue—civil rights—across an extended time period—22 years (1954–1976). They used aggregate data, utilizing 27 Gallup polls that asked the most important problem question. Thus, their measure was not a public agenda, but public concern, as determined by the percentage of Gallup poll respondents who named civil rights as the number one problem facing our country today. Again, the analysis here is placed on the issue of civil rights and not on the individuals' level of concern with civil rights.

Winter and Eyal (1981) then compared this public concern measure with the number of front-page stories in *The New York Times* that were devoted to civil rights. They found strong support for an agenda-setting effect for the civil rights issue.

Natural history studies in agenda setting, as Weaver (1994) noted, have been extremely successful and have provided substantial support for the agenda-setting hypothesis. The success of studies in this area may be attributed to the time frames examined. Agenda-setting effects, then, may be best examined across extensive time frames.

Cognitive Portrait Studies.   These studies look at single issues and individual agendas. In sharp contrast to the automaton studies, most cognitive portrait studies generally found strong support for agenda setting.

The experimental studies of Iyengar and Kinder (1987) and the quasi-experiments of Protess, Leff, Brooks, and Gordon (1985) are two good examples of research in this category.

Because Iyengar and Kinder (1987) utilized an experimental design, their operationalization of the agenda-setting effect was one of the most powerful in this area of research. They essentially constructed an index by combining responses in three areas: the subjects' personal concern for eight national issues, including the experimental treatment issues; the extent to which each issue was deserving of additional government action; and the frequency with which the subjects talked about each issue in everyday conversation. They then compared pretest scores with posttest scores. Their results yielded "striking evidence of agenda-setting" (p. 19).

Cognitive portrait studies, as Weaver (1994) argued, have been extremely successful in supporting the agenda-setting hypothesis, especially if the study employed a rigorous methodology. The experiments of Iyengar and Kinder (1987), for example, provide strong support for agenda setting, whereas the panel studies of Schoenbach (1982) and Schoenbach and Weaver (1983) provide moderate support. The one-shot, cross-sectional study of Erbring et al. (1980) produced the weakest support.

Overall Trends.   Generally, as Weaver (1994) noted, the strongest support for agenda setting involved tests in the natural history category. In general, the weakest support for agenda setting involved tests in the automaton category. In addition, experiments and panel studies tend to provide moderate to strong support for agenda setting, whereas cross-sectional studies have provided somewhat weaker support.

RECENT METHODOLOGICAL ADVANCEMENTS

Several recent studies have made significant strides in increasing the accuracy of measuring the agenda-setting effect.

Brosius and Kepplinger (1992), for example, expanded the mass persuasion measurement. For their public agenda measure, they utilized data collected by the German opinion research institute, Emnid. Their surveys asked respondents, "In your opinion, what are the most important political problems?" Respondents were then given 16 issues and were permitted to name as many of these issues as they felt were important. They then aggregated the scores to determine the number of people who mentioned each of the 16 problems for each of the time points of their study.

Because Emnid asked the same question each week throughout 1986, Brosius and Kepplinger (1992) were able to compare media coverage with public concern, using the 16 issues at 52 data points. Thus, although the aggregate data they used again placed the unit of analysis on the issue, Brosius and Kepplinger were nonetheless able to test several overall models of agenda setting—linear as well as nonlinear.

Meanwhile, Lasorsa and Wanta (1990) modified the automaton measure of agenda setting. They took the traditional most important problem question—"What is the number one problem facing our country today?"—and, instead of aggregating responses on the issues mentioned, compared the issue mentioned by each individual respondent with where the issue ranked on the media agenda. In this way, they formed a *media conformity score.*

This measure was logical on the surface. If an individual responded, "economy" and economy received the most media attention prior to the survey period, this person would score 1 on the media conformity scale.

measure if they mentioned issues that received heavy media coverage, but scored low on the media conformity measure if they mentioned issues that received little media coverage.

One problem with this measurement is readily apparent: The media conformity score was based on one response to one question. An example might illuminate this problem. Respondent A may be most concerned with the environment (and this issue might have ranked seventh on the media agenda). However, this person may also be highly concerned with the economy (which might have ranked first) and crime (which might have ranked second). Respondent B may be most concerned with the economy (which might have ranked first on the media agenda), but might also be highly concerned with government corruption (which might be ranked fifteenth) and religious freedom (which might not even make the media agenda). Given this scenario, Respondent B would score higher than Respondent A on the media conformity score. Yet, Respondent A, in actuality, demonstrated a stronger agenda-setting effect overall because of her or his concern with several issues receiving high media coverage.

Nonetheless, the media conformity score gave an indication of how influential media coverage has been on respondents' issue salience perceptions, which was the purpose behind its use.

THE DEPENDENT VARIABLE:
AGENDA-SETTING SUSCEPTIBILITY

Most of the analyses in the chapters that follow examine an *agenda-setting susceptibility* score as the dependent variable. This measure is based on respondents' stated level of concern with a list of issues, which included several issues that received extensive media coverage and other issues that received little or no coverage.

To determine the issues included in the study, the content of several news media at each of three survey sites was analyzed for the 4 weeks before the beginning of each survey period. The sites were as follows:

1. Jackson County, Illinois. The survey here was conducted in October 1990, approximately 3 weeks before the general election for governor and U.S. Senate. The area has a population of about 50,000.

2. Eugene–Springfield, Oregon. This survey was conducted in February 1994. The area has a population of about 200,000.

3. Tampa, Florida. This survey also was conducted in February
   1994. Tampa is the largest city in Hillsborough County, which
   has a population of 834,054, according to the 1990 census.

Although several researchers have utilized time lags of as short as 1 week (Wanta & Foote, 1994) and as long as 9 months (Atwood, Sohn, & Sohn, 1978), 4 weeks appears to be a logical time frame for agenda-setting effects to occur. Zucker (1978) argued that a time lag of less than 2 weeks does not allow enough time for agenda-setting effects to reach all individuals in a society and that media content of more than 4 weeks may be forgotten by media consumers. Winter and Eyal (1981) also argued for an optimal time lag of approximately 4 weeks.

All stories carried on the broadcasts of the ABC World News Tonight and the news programs from a local television station at each of the three sites were coded. ABC has had the top-rated national newscasts throughout the survey time periods. Thus, if individuals were exposed to—and thus, influenced by—a national newscast, the highest rated newscast would be the most likely source of television news information. The three local newscasts all had the top-rated viewership in their markets.

Next, content from daily newspapers serving the three areas was also analyzed. The newspapers were: the *Southern Illinoisan*, with the largest daily circulation in Jackson County, Illinois; the *Eugene Register-Guard*, with the largest daily circulation in Eugene–Springfield; and the *Tampa Tribune*, with the largest daily circulation in Tampa. Coders recorded the number of times issues were covered in all stories carried on the front pages of both the front sections and the metro sections.

The use of multiple news sources was an important consideration in our study because previous research suggested differential agenda-setting effects across the print and broadcast media (see Tipton, Haney, & Baseheart, 1975; Zucker, 1978). Thus, by using news content from multiple media, we were able to ensure an accurate gauge of the media agenda, while also allowing for comparisons across the print and broadcast media, which is detailed in a later chapter.

The number of stories dealing with the issues in the content analysis were then summed across the media. This, then, produced a media issue agenda.

The issues that received the largest number of stories in the 4 weeks before the survey periods were then chosen to be included in the study. The issues receiving the most media coverage in the Jackson County survey were the Middle East crisis, the budget deficit, the economy, and education. The issues receiving the most coverage in the Eugene–Springfield area were crime, the economy, health care, and the environment. The issues receiving the most coverage in the Tampa area were crime, international problems, the economy and the environment.

Several issues that received very little coverage were also included in our surveys for two reasons. First, including these issues helped mask the intent of the study—to gauge the magnitude of agenda-setting effects of the issues covered by the news media. Second, scores on these issues were subtracted from the media issues index to more accurately estimate the respondents' agenda-setting susceptibility. This helped guard against some respondents reporting that they were concerned with all issues, which could have biased the results.

The issues receiving low coverage that were included in the Jackson County study were international terrorism (which received three stories in the news media in the 4 weeks before the survey period), poverty/homelessness (receiving two stories), and the controversy surrounding the collapse of savings and loans (receiving two stories). The first two issues were often mentioned in the most important problem polls conducted by the Gallup organization. The collapse of the savings and loan industry was an issue that both candidates for U.S. Senate and both major party candidates for governor mentioned at one time or another; it was felt that this issue, along with the other issues included, might be important for many respondents.

The issues receiving low coverage that were included in the Eugene survey were: homelessness (which received four stories in the news media in the 4 weeks before the survey period), welfare reform (receiving two stories), and the AIDS epidemic (which received one story). The issues receiving low coverage that were included in the Tampa survey were homelessness (which received two stories in the news media in the 4 weeks before the survey period), the AIDS epidemic, and welfare reform (both of which received no coverage).

Some additional issues that were mentioned prominently in President Clinton's 1994 State of the Union address also were included. These issues were important for the analysis of the influence of factors from outside the news media that may impact on the agenda-setting process. These factors are examined in chapter 8. As with the case of the Jackson County study, other issues that appeared periodically in Gallup polls were also utilized.

To gauge the susceptibility to media agenda-setting effects, respondents were read a list of issues and asked if they were *extremely concerned, very concerned, somewhat concerned, a little concerned*, or *not at all concerned* with each issue. The order of placement for the issues that received extensive coverage and those that received little coverage was randomly determined.

The issues that received high media coverage were then weighted by the amount of coverage they received in the 4 weeks before the survey. For example, the Middle East crisis received 103 stories, or 38% of all coded stories in the Jackson County study. Thus, respondents' scores on their responses to the question dealing with their level of concern with the Middle East crisis was multiplied by .38. The scores for the issues receiving heavy media coverage were then summed to form a media issue concern score.

The concern scores for the issues receiving little coverage were then summed. This score was then subtracted from the media issue concern score. This final score, then, was used as the measure of agenda-setting susceptibility. The independent variables included in the analysis, as well as the statistical analyses employed, are detailed in later chapters.

Respondents were randomly selected using a form of random digit dialing. The first four digits were randomly selected from the area telephone directories. This method ensured that local exchanges were included. Including the fourth digit increased the likelihood that working phone numbers would be included. The final three digits then were randomly selected. The response rate across the three sites was 60%.

Interviewers were students at three universities: Southern Illinois University at Carbondale, the University of Oregon, and the University of South Florida. All interviewers went through a training session before conducting interviews. The process yielded 341 completed surveys in Jackson County, 324 in Eugene, and 244 in Tampa, providing a total of 909 respondents across the three sites.

Methodological Strengths and Weaknesses

The main strength of this study, then, is the operationalization of agenda-setting effects. Researchers previously struggled with ways of operationalizing this variable at the individual level. Hill (1985), for example, used a 5-point Likert-type scale to compute individuals' agendas. However, this method produced a large number of ties among issues, which likely confounded his results. Lasorsa and Wanta (1990) compared individuals' responses to the most important problem question with where this issue ranked on the media agenda. This media conformity score, however, dealt with only one issue.

The agenda-setting effects measure here, however, is essentially an index indicating respondents' concern with the top four issues on the media agenda. Thus, the measure employed here is a much more accurate indicator of agenda-setting effects for several reasons.

First, the measure involves four issues, not just one. A respondent extremely concerned with crime, international problems, the economy, and the environment in the Tampa sample will score higher than a respondent extremely concerned with crime, but not at all concerned with international problems, the economy, and the environment. Indeed, if the media have an agenda-setting influence, the effect implies an influence on more than one issue—actually, an entire agenda of issues. Thus, the agenda-setting susceptibility measure attempts to track the agenda-setting influence across several important issues.

Second, the measure takes into consideration the concern levels of individuals on issues not covered in the media. If individuals report that they are concerned with all issues—those receiving heavy media coverage and those receiving little coverage—this would demonstrate less media influence than it would a respondent's tendency to reply affirmatively to any and all questions. A similar problem has led to criticism in the area of cultivation theory. Does watching a lot of television programming lead to people thinking that the world is scary? Or do people think the world is scary because people who watch a lot of television tend to answer "yes" to questions? (See Hirsch, 1980, for a more detailed criticism of the cultivation theory methodology.)

High concern scores on the nonmedia issues also suggest that individuals are receiving salience cues from sources other than the news media—interpersonal communication or personal experience, for example. Thus, this would demonstrate interference with agenda-setting effects. Subtracting scores on the low-coverage issues from the concern measure for highly covered issues mitigates the influence of nonmedia sources while controlling for potential problems of affirmative answer tendencies.

It also should be noted that the methodology employed here involves tests of an automaton category of research—an examination of a set of issues at the individual level. As Weaver (1994) noted, previous automaton studies have found the weakest agenda-setting effects. However, the methodology here differs slightly from previous automaton studies.

Of concern here is not a perfect transferral of an entire media agenda, but rather a partial media agenda. In the present study, the top four issues are weighted to produce a measure that is less stringent than an examination of an entire intact agenda, but more accurate than an investigation utilizing a measure that examines one issue. Thus, here, the media agenda-setting susceptibility measure should give an accurate indication of how influential the media agenda has been on influencing the perceived salience of the top few issues that the news media have covered.

Also of concern is the fact that the data used for the majority of the analyses that follow involved surveys at three sites during two different time periods. Results across sites varied. Indeed, a separate analysis for each site produced some significant results that the initial statistical tests did not reveal. However, grouping the data from the three sites produced results that have high validity, especially because the sites here are so widely diverse, both in size and geographic region.

The two different time frames are a bit more problematic. Historical factors unique to the two time periods may have affected the findings. Agenda setting, however, is concerned with how issues rise and fall on the media and public agendas. Thus, agenda-setting research assumes that historical factors will occur at all times.

POTENTIAL MODELS OF
AGENDA-SETTING INFLUENCES

The independent variables examined here are grouped into three broad categories. They include demographics (age, education, income, gender, and race), psychological variables (political interest and media credibility), and behavioral variables (media use and interpersonal communication).

Although there could potentially be an endless number of agenda-setting models that researchers could propose and investigate, two competing models of agenda setting—the message transferral model and the knowledge activation model—are examined here.

Message Transferal Model

The first model examined is a simple message transferral process of agenda setting. Here, issue salience cues travel directly from the news media to individuals with little interference or assistance of other variables.

The basic premise behind the message transferal model is that agenda setting cannot occur without exposure to the news media. Thus, an individual's level of exposure should be the dominant factor in predicting agenda-setting susceptibility.

A simple message transferal model would argue that the higher the level of exposure to the news media, the stronger the magnitude of agenda-setting effects an individual will display. Therefore, when all variables that potentially could affect the agenda-setting process are simultaneously examined, media exposure should emerge as the most powerful.

Information, in the form of issue salience cues, is transmitted directly from the news media to media consumers. Without exposure to the news media, this transmission cannot take place.

Several previous studies have offered some support for this model. Lasorsa and Wanta (1990), for example, found that exposure to issue information strongly predicted conformity to the media agenda. Individuals with higher exposure levels, in general, were most apt to conform to the agenda of issues covered by the news media.

Knowledge Activation Model

The basic premise of the knowledge activation model is that agenda-setting effects are determined to a large degree by factors other than exposure to media messages.

In this model, media exposure does not necessarily have a strong, direct impact on individuals. Rather, media exposure activates knowledge stored in an individual's memory. The level of media exposure, then, is subordinate to other factors related to an individual's memory capacity, such as an individual's education level and/or psychological motivations.

Logically, heavy media exposure should lead to strong agenda-setting effects. Yet, of course, numerous other factors can intervene. Because mass media are so pervasive, exposure levels are relatively high for all individuals. If this were the case, exposure to the media would be relatively ineffective as a predictor of agenda-setting effects. Thus, motivational and demographic variables should be stronger predictors of agenda-setting susceptibility.

Although not discussing agenda setting specifically, Price and Tewksbury (1995) argued for a knowledge activation model of media priming and framing. They argued that news coverage influences audience evaluations through an intermediate effect on knowledge activation.

Through their news coverage, the mass media alter the accessibility of knowledge. On the one hand, individuals can only access information about issues that are being covered in the news media. Information about issues that are not covered in the media are accessible only from nonmedia sources.

On the other hand, individuals can judge the importance of media coverage only by comparing this coverage with information previously stored in their memory. Thus, information provided by the news media activates information processed at an earlier time. Factors that enhance or inhibit effective information processing within individuals—factors such as education level and interest level—therefore, should be important variables in determining the power of agenda-setting effects that they will display.

In a knowledge activation model of media agenda setting, then, exposure to news coverage is but one variable affecting the magnitude of agenda-setting effects that an individual will display. Exposure, here, serves as a catalyst for the agenda-setting process. Yet, factors that affect information processing play as important—or possibly even more important—of a role.

3

Effects of Demographic
and Psychological Variables
on Agenda Setting

Agenda setting is a complex process of social learning. An infinite number of variables can impact on this process.

This chapter examines two groups of variables that might play a role in the processing of salience cues transmitted through the news media. The variables involve demographic variables—education, income, age, race and gender—and attitudinal variables—political interest and the perceived credibility of the news media.

The agenda-setting influences of the news media do not impact on individuals uniformly. Agenda-setting effects can vary to wide degrees across different types of individuals. This chapter, then, investigates a few broad categories of variables.

THE ROLE OF DEMOGRAPHICS IN AGENDA SETTING

Examinations of demographic variables have a long and rich tradition in mass communication research, dating back to the studies conducted by Park (1925), who investigated U.S. immigrants and their use of immigrant newspapers, and Dewey (1922, 1927), who developed a psychological theory based on communication, intelligence, education, and social reform.

Demographic variables also have a wide range of applications. Researchers, for example, have applied demographic variables in causal modeling studies testing educational and occupational achievement (e. g., Duncan, Featherman, & Duncan, 1972). Kerlinger (1986) noted that the use of demographics and other social indicators have been important in several fields and have been used "to assess social conditions and social change, to monitor the achievement of governmental social goals and to study human and social conditions in order to understand and improve them" (p. 458).

However, researchers have largely ignored the role of personal characteristics in the agenda-setting process. Indeed, Hill (1985) noted the total lack of research in this area prior to his study. However, age, education, and income have all been found to be related to media usage patterns. Thus, these variables, along with race and gender, might play a role in the agenda-setting process.

Relatively little is known about how these demographic variables affect the agenda-setting process. Demographic variables, however, because they influence how individuals use and process information in the news media, could ultimately have a great deal of influence on the agenda-setting process. In other words, demographics could indirectly influence individuals' susceptibility to agenda-setting effects because these variables have been found to influence news media usage patterns.

In fact, Stone (1987) concluded that "very little in the entire realm of mass communication research is as certain as this single finding: Older, more educated and higher income individuals are the most likely newspaper clients" (p. 110). Thus, if individuals who are older, have more education, and have higher incomes also have high exposure to the news media, they should also be more susceptible to agenda-setting effects because of their media use habits. In other words, because these demographic variables have been found to influence exposure to the media—and exposure to the media is a key variable in the agenda-setting process—perhaps demographics and agenda-setting effects are also ultimately linked.

Meanwhile, several studies have found little difference in overall media consumption between men and women. The topics read by men and women, however, can differ. According to Stone (1987):

> Women comprise the majority of readership for advice columns, fashion and food sections, display ads and coupons. Men comprise the majority of readership for sports and business. But men and women do read content traditionally regarded as the other sex's domain. The overlap in readership for some of these categories is extensive. (p. 110)

Examinations of differences between racial groups in mass communication research have also produced mixed results. The question of potential differences in mass media consumption, for example, is not clear cut. Although Fielder and Tipton (1986) found that minority populations tend to use newspapers less than whites, Cranberg and Rodriguez (1994) noted that the percentages of adult minority readership mirror the overall U.S. population.

A Proposed Framework

Surprisingly few attempts have been made to examine the role that demographic variables play in the agenda-setting process. Because links have been found between demographics and media usage pat-

Hill (1985) provided a crucial first step in research in this area. Hill uncovered only one demographic variable that appeared to influence the media agenda-setting effect. He found that if respondents had some college education, they were more susceptible to agenda setting effects than individuals with lower levels of education. According to Hill's study, then, education played a role in media agenda setting.

It should be noted, however, that Hill's methodology had a significant shortcoming. Hill used a 5-point Likert-type scale to examine individuals' issue agendas. The responses to questions dealing with the perceived importance of issues were used to rank the issues. Thus, there were several ties among the issue ranks for each respondent. Because computations of Spearman rank-order correlations are hampered by tied categories, the results could have been less rigorous as they may have been with a different methodology.

Based on previous research dealing with media use demographic variables appeared to be likely to have some influence on the agenda-setting process.

Because age, education, and income have all been found to influence newspaper usage, logically agenda-setting effects should be stronger for highly educated, older individuals with high incomes—these are precisely the types of people who use the news media a great deal. In other words, because these demographic variables influence news media exposure, and because news media exposure is critical to the agenda-setting process, demographic variables should ultimately influence the magnitude of agenda-setting effects demonstrated by individuals.

On the other hand, the effects of gender and race in the agenda-setting process are less obvious. Because women and men use the news media to a similar degree, we would expect little difference between men and women on agenda-setting susceptibility. Yet, if men are more likely to first read straight news than are women (Weaver & Mauro, 1978), men may show stronger agenda-setting effects. If news is a higher priority for men, perhaps the issues covered by the media are also more important for men.

Minorities may also be less susceptible to agenda-setting effects than Whites. If minority populations tend to use newspapers less than Whites, as Fielder and Tipton (1986) concluded, and if the news is generally reported from a White male perspective (Kerner, 1968), minorities will likely have issue priorities different from Whites.

DATA ANALYSIS

The data were examined in a number of different ways. First, because age, education, and income are all interval level data, the relationships between these three variables and agenda-setting susceptibility were examined with Pearson correlations. Because gender and race produced between these three variables and agenda-setting susceptibility were examined with Pearson correlations. Because gender and race produced nominal data, these variables were examined through two analysis of variance (ANOVA) tests. Here, the mean scores for the agenda-setting susceptibility measure were compared across men and women, and across Whites and non-Whites to investigate whether any of these subgroups showed stronger agenda-setting effects.

Second, a regression analysis further examined the influence of the demographic variables on agenda-setting susceptibility. The hierarchical regression analysis examined which of the demographic variables are the best predictors of agenda-setting susceptibility.

The Minimal Effects of Demographics

Only education correlated positively with agenda-setting susceptibility ($r = .150$; $p = .000$). Thus, individuals with high education levels were more susceptible to agenda-setting effects than were individuals with low education levels. Neither age nor income were related to agenda-setting susceptibility. In addition, according to the ANOVAs, neither gender nor race were significantly related to agenda-setting susceptibility.

The regression analysis mirrored the results of the Pearson correlations. Only education was a significant predictor of agenda-setting influences ($\beta = .149$; $p = .000$). None of the other demographic variables were strong enough predictors of agenda-setting susceptibility to be entered into the regression analysis. Age ($\beta = .063$; $p = .076$) came the closest to reaching statistical significance.

Overall, then, demographic variables were relatively poor predictors of agenda-setting susceptibility. The R-Square, which notes the explained variance of the variables, shows that the demographic variables can explain only 2.7% of the variance of agenda-setting susceptibility scores. The results of these analyses point to two broad conclusions.

First, the findings suggest active information processing by individuals. In general, individuals with higher education levels are more susceptible to agenda-setting influences. Thus, the same type of individuals who are avid readers of newspapers—namely, individuals with high education levels—are most likely to be influenced by the news media. In other words, individuals who process the most media information are most susceptible to agenda setting. This finding gives some support to a simple information transferal system of media agenda setting. The more information that an individual is exposed to, the more processing that takes place and, therefore, the stronger the agenda-setting influences.

In addition, individuals with high education levels are also better prepared to understand the significance of the news content carried in the media. Because they understand what the news stories mean better than low-educated individuals, they are more likely to report concern with highly covered issues. Thus, these highly educated individuals are most susceptible to agenda-setting influences.

Second, the findings here suggest that demographics are only minimally related to agenda-setting susceptibility. Of the five demographic variables examined here, four—age, income, gender, and race—were not related to the agenda-setting susceptibility measure. Only education was found to be significantly related to the magnitude of agenda-setting effects demonstrated by respondents.

Overall, then, other variables—psychological and/or behavioral variables—may have intervened between demographics and agenda-setting susceptibility. As seen later, this may have been the case.

Individuals' Attitudes in Agenda Setting

People have a wide range of opinions regarding the job performed by the news media. Some believe the media are biased in the way they cover certain topics. Others believe the news media do a good job of telling both sides of issues. People also have a wide range of interest levels in political news. Some are news junkies who actively seek out vast amounts of political information. Others are chronic know nothings who have priorities other than keeping informed about their community's issues.

This analysis involves the attitudes of individuals and how they relate to susceptibility to agenda-setting effects. Two attitudinal variables are examined here. First, media credibility is examined. It is logical to assume that if people view the news media positively, they will also expose themselves to the media often and be more strongly influenced by the media's messages.

Second, political interest is examined. If people have a high interest in political news, it is likely that they will seek out information about politics by exposing themselves to the media often and, again, will be more susceptible to agenda-setting influences of the media.

Attitudinal variables should play important roles in the agenda-setting process. The mental processing of issue information contained in the news media is likely to be influenced by psychological factors inherent within individuals. Indeed, the psychological makeup of individuals puts them in certain moods that might motivate them to use the news media, which in turn might leave them open to the potential influences of the messages.

THEORETICAL BACKGROUND

Of concern here are two psychological variables that may influence the magnitude of agenda-setting effects demonstrated by individuals: political interest and perceived credibility of the media.

Political interest, of course, should indicate individuals' motivation for exposing themselves to issue information. Early agenda-setting studies pointed to an individual's need for orientation. This need for orientation was based on the presupposition that individuals feel some motivation to be familiar with their surroundings. Individuals, then, use the mass media to fill in details about the world that they feel they must know, to orient themselves to find their way around in their world.

The perceived credibility of the news media also should play a role in the agenda-setting process. As Hovland and his colleagues argued, how we view a messenger affects the ability of the messenger to influence us (e. g., Hovland, Janis, & Kelley, 1953). Highly credible sources have a more powerful effect on individuals than do noncredible sources. Thus, if individuals believe the media are highly credible, they will likely demonstrate strong agenda-setting effects.

Political Interest

Individuals differ greatly in the amount of interest they show in the U.S. political process. Some demonstrate keen interests in political events and thus, are both heavy media users and frequent participants in interpersonal discussions about politics. Other individuals are far less interested. For them, politics is an extremely low priority in their lives. Many are so disinterested that they do not even bother to vote.

Political interest, it would appear, should be highly correlated with both media use and agenda-setting susceptibility. High interest in politics should motivate individuals into using the news media to gain information. It follows, then, that high media exposure will lead to strong agenda-setting effects.

Indeed, political interest has been found to be related to media usage. As Stone (1987) noted, "People will not attend to messages that have no perceived interest value for them" (p. 129). High media users also feel a strong civic duty to keep informed about the day's news events and tend to be leaders in a community (McCombs & Poindexter, 1983). Thus, high political interest and involvement are often associated with high media use.

McManus (1994) argued that the nature of television news may be partly to blame for the increasing apathy shown by the general public. He wrote:

Such citizens don't take seriously the burden of informed democratic participation in large measure because the news portrays politics as irrelevant to their lives. Consequently, these citizens are blindsided by the results of political processes they don't understand. They become victims. Their informational powerlessness builds apathy. And that makes them both less eager and less able to comprehend serious reporting. (p. 197)

Kinder and Sears (1985) also noted that Americans typically pay casual and intermittent attention to political issues and are often extremely ignorant of the details pertaining to these issues. Meanwhile, political interest has also been examined in a number of agenda-setting studies. They have often produced contradictory results.

MacKuen and Coombs (1981) argued that the more attentive the individual is, the more attention he or she will pay to media messages and the more susceptible he or she will be to agenda-setting effects. Indeed, MacKuen and Coombs (1981) and Erbring et al. (1980) found that the more interested individuals were in political issues, the more susceptible they were to agenda-setting effects.

An active processing model of agenda-setting influence would support this position. In other words, the positive relationship between interest and agenda-setting effects would be expected if individuals are active processors of media messages. Individuals actively seek out information about important issues based on the needs of each individual. Many times, the source of information is the news media. By actively seeking out information from the news media, individuals are exposed to media messages and the agenda-setting influences contained in the messages. Thus, high interest in politics may ultimately lead to high agenda-setting effects.

However, the evidence for this position is unclear. Mullins (1973) found no relationship between interest and media agenda setting. McLeod et al. (1974), Winter (1981), and Weaver et al. (1981) found that the most interested individuals were less susceptible to media influence. They posited two explanations.

First, individuals highly interested in political issues are also likely to be highly involved in politics within a community. Therefore, with high community involvement, these individuals have additional sources other than the news media that they can gain information from on important issues. In other words, individuals who demonstrate strong community ties do not need the news media to tell them which issues are important. They learn about important issues firsthand through their involvement in their communities.

Second, individuals highly interested in political issues may have more highly developed defense mechanisms. That is, these individuals may not passively accept the media's ranking of issues as their own, but instead may bring their own interests and background into the agenda-setting process. These individuals, then, may be more critical in their personal ranking of political issues, despite the level of media coverage that the issues receive and the individuals' level of media exposure. Individuals with low interests in politics, on the other hand, may be more passive in their processing of media information and, therefore, may not be as critical in their evaluations of media coverage.

Finally, Iyengar, Peters, and Kinder (1982) also found a negative relationship between attention and agenda-setting effects. Through two experiments, they found that the more involved and attentive individuals were, the less they were affected by television news agenda. Conversely, the less attentive individuals were most affected by issue coverage of television news. Thus, the role that political interest plays in the agenda-setting process is unclear. Research in this area is needed to clear up these contradictory results.

If agenda setting is a process in which individuals are active participants, interest in political matters should be positively related to agenda-setting effects. Logically, if individuals actively seek out information on political issues because they are interested in these issues, they will expose themselves heavily to media messages to obtain this information. Thus, if individuals are highly interested in political issues, they will expose themselves to media information and thus, become susceptible to agenda-setting influences.

Motivational factors in the agenda-setting process were first proposed in the notion of the need for orientation. Weaver (1977) noted that three major factors contribute to a person's need for orientation: interest in a message's content; uncertainty about the subject of the message; and the effort required to attend to the message. Early research on the need for orientation concentrated on the first two factors, with the assumption that the third factor—effort—was a constant. Their reasoning was that because media messages are readily available to nearly all individuals, a great deal of exhaustive effort is really not necessary to find media messages.

A need for orientation typology developed by McCombs and Weaver (1985) is shown in Fig. 3.1. The typology is based on the assumption that the factors of relevance and uncertainty are both related to the need for orientation. High relevance and high uncertainty lead to a high need for orientation. High relevance and low uncertainty or low relevance and high uncertainty lead to a moderate need for orientation. Low relevance and low uncertainty produces a low need for orientation.

For individuals with a strong interest in politics, news about politics will be highly relevant. Thus, political interest either produces a moderate or a high need for orientation, depending upon the individual's level of uncertainty. If need for orientation leads directly to agenda-setting effects, then a high interest in political news will also lead to strong agenda-setting effects. Thus, according to the model of need for orientation, political interest should lead to high agenda-setting effects because interest in politics should mean that political news is highly relevant to the individual.

Media Credibility

Individuals can have a wide range of opinions about the news media. Some paint the media as biased, complaining that they constantly try

Uncertainty

	Low	High
Low	Low Need for Orientation	Moderate Need for Orientation
High	Moderate Need for Orientation	High Need for Orientation

Relevance

FIG. 3.1. Need for orientation typology. From "Toward a Merger of Gratifications and agenda Setting Research," by McCombs and Weaver, 1985. In Media Gratifications Research, by K. E. Rosengren, L. A. Wenner, & P. Palmgreen (Eds.), 1985, Beverly Hills, CA: Sage. Copyright © 1985 by Sage. Reprinted with permission.

to slant public opinion to the left or to the right. Others think reporters do a competent job of informing society of the day's events.

Recently, leaders in the news media have lamented a *credibility crisis*. Members of the public in increasing numbers are doubting the believability of the media generally and newspapers specifically.

Credibility of sources of information has been widely explored in many different disciplines. Important early work in this area was conducted by Hovland and his associates (e. g., Hovland et al., 1953). Hovland et al. found that source credibility was an important factor in determining the relative influence a message had on individuals. They suggested two components as influencing credibility: expertness and trustworthiness.

Research into the credibility of the mass media, however, has faced a number of conceptual problems. Singletary (1976), in examining 16 factors, pointed to the difficulty of applying credibility to the news media. He concluded that source credibility is "highly complex and somewhat undifferentiated" (p. 318).

More recently, Gaziano and McGrath (1986) proposed a 12-item index for examining media credibility. Although their analysis found that all 12 items loaded on a single factor, they suggested that their index could be subdivided into narrower elements.

Rimmer and Weaver (1987) used a subset of the Gaziano and McGrath index to apply credibility to media use. They found that television or newspaper credibility did not correlate with frequency of use, but did correlate with media choice, indicating that credibility influences the choice of media used, but not how often individuals will use a particular medium.

Finally, Meyer (1989) developed a credibility index consisting of two factors. From his factor analysis, two useful scales measuring credibility emerged: one dealing with believability, the other with community affiliation. Believability, closely aligned with Hovland's trustworthiness criterion, is based on the assumption that news media need to offer accurate and unbiased information. The affiliation index was based on newspaper editors' concerns that media need to maintain harmony and a leadership status in a community. This chapter applies the two credibility measurements developed by Meyer (1989)—believability and affiliation—in an agenda-setting framework.

A Proposed Framework

The two psychological variables examined here should be positively related to agenda-setting susceptibility.

• Political interest. A high interest in politics would indicate a high need for orientation by an individual. If an individual has a high need for information, they will likely turn to the media for this information often. Thus, individuals with a strong interest in politics may be highly susceptible to agenda-setting effects because of their need to satisfy their interest in politics.

• Media credibility. Attitudes toward the source of a message should the message's effectiveness. If a highly credible source is providing information, an individual will likely think that the information, as with the source, are very credible. Credible information will be processed more efficiently and carefully by individuals, and thus, have a stronger impact on an individual than information for a untrustworthy source. Therefore, if individuals view the news media to be highly credible, they should demonstrate stronger agenda-setting effects.

DATA ANALYSIS

Political interest was determined by responses to one item. The question asked to respondents: How interested are you in political issues? Would you say you are extremely interested, very interested, somewhat interested, a little interested, or not at all interested in political issues?

The political interest question was worded slightly differently for the Jackson County survey. Here, respondents were asked: "How interested would you say you are in following the campaign for U.S. Senate and Illinois governor this year? Would you say you are extremely interested, very interested, somewhat interested, a little interested, or not at all interested?"

To examine how credible the respondents viewed the news media, two indexes were formed, based on the research of Meyer (1989). The first, which was based on the believability of the news media, consisted of four items. Respondents were asked if they *strongly agree, somewhat agree*, are *undecided, somewhat disagree*, or *strongly disagree* with four statements: "News organizations such as newspapers and television news try to manipulate public opinion;" "News organizations often fail to get all of the facts straight;" "News organizations often don't deal fairly with all sides of a political or social issue;" and "News organizations do a poor job of separating facts from opinions." The responses were coded in such a way that higher the score, the more credible the respondents felt the media were. The four responses were then summed to form a *media believability* index. The Cronbach's alpha for the believability index was .79.

The second index, which was based on the community affiliation of the news media, consisted of three items (Meyer, 1989). Respondents again were asked if they *strongly agree, somewhat agree*, are *undecided, somewhat disagree*, or *strongly disagree* to three statements: "News organizations are concerned with the community's well-being;" "News organizations watch out for your interests;" and "News organizations are concerned mainly about the public welfare." Again, responses were coded to ensure that the higher the score, the more credible the individual felt the media were. The responses were then summed to form a *community affiliation index*. The Cronbach's alpha for the affiliation index was .77.

As with the previous analyses, the relationships between the variables were first examined with Pearson correlations. Both political interest and media credibility should be positively related to agenda-setting susceptibility. Thus, we would expect positive and significant correlations for the variables examined here.

The variables were further examined through a regression analysis. Again, the regression analysis allows for a comparison across variables. Thus, a regression tells us which of the variables is the best predictor of agenda-setting susceptibility.

The Powerful Influence of Political Interest

Table 3.1 lists the Pearson correlations examining the relationships between the psychological variables and agenda-setting susceptibility. As the results show, the correlation for political interest was highly significant ($p = .000$). Both of the media credibility measures also produced statistically significant correlations with the agenda-setting susceptibility measure.

Table 3.2 shows the regression analysis results, examining the influence of the psychological variables on agenda-setting susceptibility. Here, political interest again was the strongest predictor of agenda-setting susceptibility. Perceived community affiliation was also a significant predictor. Media believability was not entered into the final regression analysis.

The results here show that the strongest correlation with the dependent variable of agenda-setting susceptibility involves political interest ($r = .287; p < .001$). Thus, the more interested individuals were in politics, the stronger the agenda-setting effects they displayed.

This lends support to the notion of an individual's need for orientation. As Weaver (1977) argued, interest in a message's content—namely, the news media's coverage of issues—leads to a strong need for orientation. Interest in politics provides individuals with the motivation to seek out information on issues from the news media. Thus, interest in politics, although likely impacting on individuals' news media usage patterns, ultimately leads to agenda-setting effects.

The statistically significant influence of this attitudinal variable underscores the active processing of information by individuals. If individuals are interested in politics, they turn to the news media for information and, thus, are more accessible to agenda-setting effects. Individuals with low interests in politics are less likely to actively seek out information on important issues and, thus, are less susceptible to agenda-setting influences.

Therefore, these findings suggest that agenda setting is a process in which individuals are active participants. Individuals actively seek out

TABLE 3.1
Pearson Correlations Examining the Relationships Between Psychological Variables
and Agenda-Setting Susceptibility

Variable	Pearson r	Significance
Political interest	.287	.000
Community affiliation	.190	.000
Media believability	.071	.036

TABLE 3.2
Regression Analysis Results for the Influence of Psychological Variables
on Agenda-Setting Susceptibility

Variable	Beta	Significance
Political interest	.293	.000
Community affiliation	.201	.000
Media believability	.023	.509

Note. Multiple $R = .349$; R-Square $= .122$; Adjusted R-Square $= .119$.

information on political issues because they are interested in these issues and expose themselves heavily to media messages to obtain this information. This exposure leaves them susceptible to agenda-setting influences.

The credibility variables, although not as powerful as political interest, also show a relationship with agenda-setting susceptibility, with one exception. Although both the community affiliation index and the believability index were correlated with agenda-setting susceptibility, only the community affiliation index was a strong enough predictor of agenda-setting susceptibility to be entered into the regression analysis after the political interest variable was accounted for. Thus, respondents' views of the source of issue information—their perceptions regarding the credibility of the news media—played a secondary role in agenda setting. Respondents' attitudes toward the message itself—their level of interest in the information—was much more important.

The lack of power for the media believability index could be attributed to a number of factors. First, the perceived believability of the media may simply play a limited role in the agenda-setting process. Individuals may not consider the believability of the source of the message when contemplating the perceived importance of issues covered in the media. Indeed, an individual may think the media are unbelievable, unfair, and biased, yet he or she may become highly concerned with issues covered in the same media.

Moreover, it would be difficult for individuals to ignore all media coverage of issues. It may be as McCombs (1981) has suggested—that the mass media are so pervasive that it would be nearly impossible to avoid all contact with the media. Because individuals cannot avoid all contact with the news media, almost all individuals are susceptible to some level of agenda-setting influence—including those individuals who believe the media are not very credible. Thus, media content, and media agenda-setting influences, are so pervasive that attitudes about the source of the content—the media themselves—are unimportant.

With interpersonal communication channels reinforcing media messages, discussions with peers and family may expose individuals to media messages even if these individuals are highly critical of the media. In other words, a two-step flow of information may influence even individuals who avoid all contact with the news media, including individuals who are highly critical of the job journalists do.

Recently, Weimann (1994) found support for a two-step flow of agenda-setting effects. He found that *influentials*, individuals who are highly interested in political news and high media users, are first influenced by the news media. These influentials pass on the agenda-setting effect to opinion followers. Thus, almost all individuals, even low media users, get some exposure to agenda-setting influences.

In addition, these results support the findings of Rimmer and Weaver (1987). Similar to the findings here, Rimmer and Weaver found that television or newspaper credibility did not correlate with frequency of use. Thus, perhaps this psychological variable simply is unrelated to agenda-setting susceptibility or media use.

However, community affiliation was correlated with agenda-setting susceptibility and was a significant predictor of agenda-setting influences. Thus, if individuals believed the media were looking out for the community's welfare, they also believed the issues covered in the media were important. That is, if individuals believe the media are highly affiliated with society, they tend to believe the issues covered are in the best interest of society. Thus, individuals who positively view the media will be directly influenced by the messages that the media transmit, regardless of other factors.

Additional Political Variables

To further examine the role of attitudinal factors in the agenda-setting process, two additional variables were examined: political philosophy and party affiliation.

On the surface, neither one of these two variables appear to be theoretically linked to the concept of agenda setting. Indeed, the agenda-setting hypothesis does not address the question of political philosophy. Agenda setting posits that media coverage influences issue concern, not the side of an issue—whether it be conservative or liberal—that the media or media consumer assume. Although the mass media may provide extensive coverage of a certain issue, the coverage may not necessarily influence an individual's stance on the issue. As Cohen (1963) argued, the press may not necessarily tell us what to think, yet it is stunningly successful in telling us what to think about.

The following example illuminates this relationship. A newspaper series advocates the passage of strict gun control laws—a liberal side of an issue. According to the agenda-setting hypothesis, media consumers will believe that gun control is an important issue, but they will not necessarily believe that strict laws are needed. Indeed, if they are conservative, and are opposed to gun control laws, the media coverage may merely reinforce their stance on the issue by pointing out arguments with which they do not agree. In the meantime, media consumers' exposure to the gun control series will raise the perceived importance of the issue on their personal agenda.

Similarly, party affiliation should have little influence in the agenda-setting process. Republicans should not differ from Democrats on their susceptibility to agenda-setting effects, although they obviously differ on issue stances.

However, the liberal sides of issues hold more drama. For example, a story about a state budget deficit is less compelling than a story about the adverse effect of state funding cuts on social programs. Thus, coverage of more liberal issues, such as the environment or education, may have a stronger agenda-setting effect on liberal individuals. Such coverage may reinforce an individual's concern with these issues. Indeed, several of the issues included in the agenda-setting susceptibility measure were liberal issues, such as health care and the environment, although these issues were balanced with several conservative issues, such as the budget deficit and crime.

Table 3.3 shows the Pearson correlations for the two political variables. Political philosophy correlated with agenda-setting susceptibility. The more liberal a respondent professed to be, the more likely they were to be concerned with issues covered in the media. Thus, liberal respondents showed stronger agenda-setting effects. Party affiliation, however, was not related to agenda-setting susceptibility; Republicans and Democrats showed a similar level of agenda-setting influences.

The weak role these two variables play in agenda setting is further demonstrated in Table 3.4. Neither political philosophy nor party affiliation was a strong enough predictor to be entered into the regression analysis after political interest and the two credibility measures

TABLE 3.3

Pearson Correlations Examining the Relationships Between Political Philosophy and Party Affiliation and Agenda-Setting Susceptibility

Variable	Pearson r	Significance
Political philosophy	.149	.008
Party affiliation	-.024	.496

Note. Political philosophy was coded as ranging from 1 (*strongly conservative*) to 5 (*strongly liberal*). Thus, the significant correlation suggests that the strongly liberal respondents were the most susceptible to agenda-setting influences. Party affiliation was coded as 1 (*strongly Republican*) to 5 (*strongly Democratic*).

TABLE 3.4

Regression Analysis Results for the Influence of Political Philosophy, Party Affiliation and the Previously Tested Psychological Variables on Agenda-Setting Susceptibility

Variable	Beta	Significance
Political interest	.336	.000
Community affiliation	.205	.000
Media believability	.120	.042
Political philosophy	.067	.234
Party affiliation	.028	.622

Note. Multiple R = .486; R-Square = .236; Adjusted R-Square = .223.

were accounted for. Thus, political philosophy and party affiliation were weak predictors of agenda-setting susceptibility.

CONCLUSIONS

Overall, the psychological measures employed here in the initial analysis appear to be directly related to agenda-setting susceptibility. Highly interested individuals who view the news media in a positive light are highly susceptible to agenda-setting influences. Therefore, psychological variables appear to be important factors in the agenda-setting process. Respondents' attitudes play an important role in determining how individuals view and process information transmitted by the news media. However, political attitudes, such as party affiliation and political philosophy have a very limited influence on the agenda-setting process; motivations are more important.

4

Effects of Behavioral Variables on Agenda Setting

An active processing model of agenda setting would assume that what people do with media messages plays an important role in the development of issue salience. If individuals do not expose themselves to the news media—either directly or indirectly through interpersonal communication channels—they will have no way of learning the relative importance of issues covered in the media. If individuals do not discuss political issues with others, they will not reinforce these media messages with information from other sources.

Behavioral variables, then, logically should be important aspects of agenda setting. Studies examining the role of behavior variables in agenda setting, however, have often produced mixed results.

Indeed, studies investigating the role of interpersonal communication in the agenda-setting process—as with those investigating political interest—have produced widely contradictory results. Various studies have found that interpersonal communication enhances agenda-setting effects (McLeod et al. 1974; Mullins 1973), inhibits agenda-setting effects (Atwater et al., 1985; Erbring et al., 1980 Weaver, Auh, Stehla, & Wilhoit, 1975;), or has no effect at all (Hong & Shemer, 1976; Lasorsa & Wanta, 1990). Few contingent conditions in agenda setting have drawn more attention from researchers with such little agreement in their results.

A few researchers have attempted to make sense of this puzzle. Winter (1981) blamed the contradictory findings on a lack of consistency in methodologies. He noted that studies concerned with interpersonal communication have employed single-issue and multiple-issue designs, while examining student, metropolitan, national, and international populations. Wanta and Wu (1992) found that the role of interpersonal communication in the agenda-setting process was contingent on whether the discussions involved issues covered in the media or issues ignored by the media.

Meanwhile, media exposure has been relatively stable as a strong predictor of agenda-setting effects. Media exposure, however, has often been taken as a given in agenda-setting research. Because media messages are so pervasive, exposure to the media has been excluded for many agenda-setting studies. Thus, even this variable needs further attention.

THEORETICAL BACKGROUND

Of concern in this chapter are two behavioral variables that may influence the magnitude of agenda-setting effects demonstrated by individuals: interpersonal communication and news media usage.

Interpersonal communication should play an important role in the agenda-setting process in two ways. First, discussions of political issues may reinforce media messages for high media users. Let's return to the high media user discussed in chapter 2. Here, the attorney reads and processes media messages, but by discussing the same issues with others—coworkers, family members, and friends—he or she will get a second exposure to the issues covered in the media. Thus, high interpersonal communication leads to high agenda-setting susceptibility.

Second, interpersonal discussions expose low media users indirectly to media messages. Again, by using one of the two individuals discussed in chapter 2, this point is illustrated. The unemployed construction worker may not be directly exposed to issue coverage because of his low media use, but high interpersonal communication gives this person some exposure to issues, that is, if the discussions deal with issues covered in the media. Therefore, even with little media exposure, some individuals are indirectly exposed to media messages through their interpersonal discussions.

Meanwhile, media exposure is the basis behind the agenda-setting hypothesis. Media coverage of issues needs some level of exposure from individuals to produce an agenda-setting effect. The higher the media exposure, the more often individuals see the salience cues transmitted by the media. Media exposure, then, should directly influence the individuals' susceptibility to agenda-setting influences.

INTERPERSONAL COMMUNICATION

Research examining the role of interpersonal communication in the agenda-setting function of the press has been a tangled mass of contradictory results. Although most studies have supported the basic agenda-setting hypothesis (that members of the public learn cues as to the relative importance of issues from the coverage these issues receive in the press), the effect of interpersonal discussions on the agenda-setting process remains unclear.

On the one hand, interpersonal communication in some cases has been found to enhance agenda-setting effects (e. g., McLeod et al., 1974; Mullins, 1973). Interpersonal communication, indeed, often involves the discussion of items that people read in the newspaper or saw on newscasts. People often talk about articles they read in the newspaper or stories they saw on the newscasts. Whether it be a general comment about crime—"All I see on the news is crime after crime after crime"—or a specific comment about international problems—"Did you see the story last night about the terrorist bombings in the Middle East?"—interpersonal discussions can reinforce salience cues transmitted by the news media.

On the other hand, interpersonal communication has also been found to inhibit agenda-setting effects (see Atwater et al., 1985; Erbring et al., 1980; and Weaver et al., 1975). Interpersonal discussions obviously do not always involve political issues covered in the news media. Individuals may discuss issues that received no media coverage, but for some reason concern them greatly (e.g., unemployment in the construction industry). Thus, interpersonal communication can give individuals salience cues that conflict with salience cues transmitted by the news media. Interpersonal communication can then involve a source of information that is different from the information contained in the news media, thus interfering with normal media agenda-setting influences.

Yet, other studies have found interpersonal communication to have no effect at all on the agenda-setting influence of the press (Hong & Shemer, 1976; Lasorsa & Wanta, 1990). Lasorsa and Wanta (1990), for example, argued that personal involvement with issues and mass media usage patterns are stronger predictors of agenda-setting influences than interpersonal communication. Interpersonal discussions are but one source of information about issues that may conflict or reinforce salience cues transmitted by the news media.

Meanwhile, Winter (1981) blamed the contradictory findings on a lack of consistency in methodologies. Two studies of interpersonal communication and agenda setting demonstrate this inconsistency. Mullins (1977) examined a student population during the 1972 presidential election, whereas Atwater et al. (1985) studied a more general population but investigated only one issue (the environment). The Mullins study found interpersonal communication enhanced agenda-setting effects, but the Atwater et al. study found exactly the opposite: Interpersonal communication inhibited agenda-setting influences.

Wanta and Wu (1992) used two key aspects to clear up the ambiguity of previous findings. First, their measurement of interpersonal communication was issue specific—that is, respondents were asked their level of interpersonal discussion on specific issues chosen by the investigators. Second, the issues under investigation were placed into two categories: mass-mediated issues—those receiving extensive coverage in the news media prior to the survey period; and nonmediated issues—those receiving little or no coverage in the news media prior to the survey period. They found that for mass-mediated issues, interpersonal communication reinforced the media's issue coverage. Thus, in this case, interpersonal communication led to higher agenda-setting effects. For nonmediated issues, however, they found that interpersonal communication interfered with the media's issue coverage. In this case, interpersonal communication led to lower agenda-setting effects by increasing the salience of issues that were not covered in the news media.

The relationship between mass and interpersonal communication has been examined in a number of settings. Roling, Ascroft, and WaChege (1976) suggested that interpersonal channels are filled with information that the news media either do not or cannot provide, such as rumors, slanders, and other often inaccurate and internally inconsistent information. Although people generally prefer the news media over interpersonal channels and tend to believe the media more (Chaffee, 1982; Edelstein & Tefft, 1974), the news media often cannot keep up with the demand for opinion guidance, and people consequently turn to interpersonal sources (Coleman, 1957). In addition, some people will try to reduce uncertainty by consulting people with different political viewpoints. Interpersonal communication, indeed, is an extremely important information source for many people. The importance of interpersonal communication was the chief concern leading to examinations of the two-step flow of communication proposed by Katz and Lazarsfeld (1955).

Weimann (1994) recently re-examined the notion of a two-step flow of mass communication influence. Based on results from recent surveys conducted in Germany, Weimann suggested that the mass media demonstrated a stronger short-term agenda-setting effect on opinion leaders, but over longer periods of time, the magnitude of agenda-setting effects were strongest for opinion followers. Thus, the findings demonstrate renewed support for a two-step flow of media influence. In other words, the agenda-setting influence of the press first affects influentials. Opinion followers are thus influenced by the media at a much later time, after the media influence is filtered through the opinion leaders. Indeed, Weimann's findings of differential agenda-setting effects among opinion leaders and followers seems eminently logical.

Overall, however, the effect of interpersonal communication on the agenda-setting function of the press has continued to confound researchers. Several explanations for the contradictory results have been proposed, the following are included:

• Different media impact on interpersonal discussions to differing degrees. Shaw and McCombs (1977), for example, suggested that interpersonal agendas, which include issues that people talk about, may be more affected by television, whereas intrapersonal agendas, which include issues that people think are important, may be more affected by newspapers. Television and interpersonal discussions may interact.

• Timing may be a factor in the relationship between interpersonal discussions and agenda setting. McLeod et al. (1974) argued that interpersonal communication plays a greater role later in political campaigns when newspapers decline as an agenda-setting source.

• Interpersonal communication may be an intervening variable between media and personal agendas. Atwood et al. (1978), examining *community discussion* as a dependent variable, found that newspapers influenced what people talk about, but were not the only source of topics. Hong and Shemer (1976) thus believed that interpersonal communication may either facilitate or reduce the importance of issues.

• The history of the issue being discussed can play a role in the effectiveness of the interpersonal communication. Erbring et al. (1980) concluded that interpersonal communication is essential to help people make sense of news media content. They found that informal communication increases issue salience for new issues, but not for long-standing issues.

Overall, then, the contradictory findings of previous studies suggest that interpersonal communication can enhance agenda-setting effects in some cases, while inhibiting the effects in others.

EXPOSURE TO MEDIA MESSAGES

Exposure to the mass media, as mentioned earlier, has often been taken for granted in agenda-setting research. McCombs (1981), in explaining the concept of *need for orientation*, suggested that the mass media are so pervasive that it is nearly impossible to avoid all contact with them.

Studies examining exposure have generally found significant correlations between level of exposure and strength of agenda-setting effects. Lasorsa and Wanta (1990), for example, found that media exposure and attention to media messages were strong predictors of conformity to the mass media agenda. Similarly, MacKuen and Coombs (1981) found an individual's level of media exposure was highly correlated with agenda-setting effects.

Similarly, McClure and Patterson (1976) found that the level of newspaper exposure was significantly related to issue salience. Although they did not find the same pattern for television news, they suggested that the influence of the level of exposure to television news may have been masked by the viewer's level of newspaper exposure. Thus, exposure to media messages across different news media are not uniform.

Finally, Mullins (1977) found support for an *individual practice* hypothesis for young voters. Hypothesizing that the level of exposure to the mass media is a form of learning practice, Mullins found that the more young voters see or read the news, the more they absorbed the media issues as their own.

A Proposed Framework

The logic of the agenda-setting hypothesis posits that individuals learn the relative importance of issues from the coverage these issues receive in the news media. According to the agenda-setting hypothesis, those issues receiving extensive coverage in the news media should be perceived as important to individuals. In addition, high news consumers should be more susceptible to agenda-setting influences than low news consumers because of the repetition of exposure to media messages by the high consumers.

However, if individuals take the issue salience cues they received from the media and discuss these same issues with others, the interpersonal communication will reinforce the media agenda-setting effects. In other words, issues that receive extensive media coverage and are also discussed often by an individual, are perceived to be even more important than issues that receive extensive coverage but are not discussed by individuals. Hence, in this instance, interpersonal communication will enhance media agenda-setting effects.

Mediated issues, moreover, are also perceived as important by individuals who have not been exposed to media content, but have been exposed to interpersonal discussions dealing with these issues. This is the basic notion of the *two-step flow of communication* (Lazarsfeld, Berelson, & Gaudet, 1948), in which media content is passed on by media users to nonmedia users. Although the notion of the two-step flow of communication has been criticized, Rogers and Shoemaker (1971) concluded that the combination of the mass media and interpersonal communication is the most effective way to reach people with new ideas and persuade them to utilize new innovations. Thus, if interpersonal communication reinforces media messages, the higher the level of interpersonal discussions that individuals take part in, the more susceptible they will be to agenda-setting influences.

Exposure to media messages should also be highly related to agenda-setting susceptibility. The more individuals expose themselves to issue information contained in the news media, the more they are influenced by issue coverage. Thus, high media exposure leads to strong agenda-setting effects. This was the basic relationship first stated in the early agenda-setting studies (McCombs & Shaw, 1972).

In its most basic form, the agenda-setting hypothesis is based on a simple message transferal model. The media provide issue information. Exposure to the media messages determines how much of the issue information is transferred from the media to the individual. High exposure means extensive information transferal, and thus the potential for strong agenda-setting effects. The relationship between exposure and agenda-setting effects, then, is likely to be linear.

DATA ANALYSIS

A single-item question was used to measure the respondents' interpersonal communication levels. Respondents were asked: "How often would you say that you discuss political issues with others?" "Would you say you very often, quite often, occasionally, rarely, or never discuss political issues with others?"

The interpersonal communication measure was different in the Jackson County survey. Here, respondents were asked how often they discussed each mediated and nonmediated issue in the last week—*more than once a day, about once a day, a few times in the last week, once or twice in the last week,* or *not at all*. The issues were placed in the same order as the issue concern section of the questionnaire. The interpersonal communication scores for the mediated issues were then summed to form a mediated interpersonal communication index (α = .75).

Three items measured exposure to the news media. Respondents were asked how many days in the past week they read a newspaper. The levels of exposure to national and local television news broadcasts were measured similarly. The three exposure items were then summed and the Cronbach's alpha was .68.

Again, the relationships between the variables were examined through Pearson correlations and regression analyses.

TABLE 4.1
Pearson Correlations Examining the Relationships Between Behavioral Variables and
Agenda-Setting Susceptibility

Variable	Pearson r	Significance
Interpersonal communication	.143	.000
Media exposure	.084	.014

TABLE 4.2
Regression Analysis Results for the Influence of Behaviorcal Variables on Agenda-Setting
Susceptibility

Variable	Beta	Significance
Interpersonal communication	.123	.000
Media exposure	.057	.106

Note. Multiple $R = .149$; R-Square $= .022$; Adjusted R-Square $= .019$.

Support for the Positive Influence of Behavioral Variables. As Table 4.1 shows, both behavioral variables were significantly related to agenda-setting susceptibility. The higher the exposure to the news media, the stronger the agenda-setting effects demonstrated by respondents ($p = .0014$). Similarly, the higher the interpersonal communication respondents took part in, the stronger the agenda-setting effects ($p = .000$).

Table 4.2 lists the regression analysis results examining the influence of the behavioral variables on agenda-setting susceptibility. The strength of the interpersonal communication variable is readily apparent here. Interpersonal communication was such a powerful predictor that media exposure did not significantly add to the explained variance of agenda-setting susceptibility. The explained variance here was only 2.2%.

Overall, the results here show that the two behavioral variables were significantly related to agenda-setting susceptibility. Individuals who often discussed issues with others and/or were high media users were more likely to demonstrate strong agenda-setting effects.

If individuals are active processors of information in the agenda-setting process, they will demonstrate agenda-setting effects based on their previous behaviors. As expected, media use and interpersonal communication were related to the agenda-setting susceptibility measure employed here. In other words, according to the Pearson correlations, the more individuals were exposed to the news media and the more they discussed issues with others, the more susceptible they were to agenda-setting effects. Interpersonal communication was also a significant predictor of agenda-setting susceptibility in the regression analysis.

The findings demonstrate that individuals who are active processors of the news—those who often read newspapers, watch television news, and talk to others about the news—are more susceptible to agenda-setting effects than passive processors. In other words, agenda setting is a dynamic process in which individuals actively process information gathered from information sources. The more exposure to issue information, the more information that is processed. The more information that is processed on certain political issues, the more important these issues will be perceived to be by individuals.

The findings show further support for a simple message transferal model of agenda-setting. According to the Pearson correlations, the more individuals are exposed to the news media, the more likely the information contained in the news media coverage will get transferred to these individuals. Thus, media exposure ultimately leads to strong agenda-setting effects.

In addition, interpersonal communication plays an important reinforcement role in the agenda-setting process. By discussing political issues covered in the media, individuals are exposed to two sources of information on the issues—the mass media and other people. The interpersonal communication reinforces the information carried in the news media messages. Thus, individuals are highly susceptible to agenda-setting influences when they expose themselves to media messages and discuss the issues with others.

Despite such conclusive evidence, the findings here leave a number of questions unanswered. First, as Rogers and Shoemaker (1971) and Wanta and Wu (1992) found, the combination of media exposure and interpersonal communication simultaneously leads to the most effective method of communication. Thus, interpersonal communication may interact with media coverage to produce issue salience that is higher than would be expected from isolated interpersonal communication or isolated media coverage. Such interaction could be due to three factors. One factor is the individual's use of interpersonal channels to compare their perceived salience of issues with others. Interpersonal communication then decreases uncertainty on the level of salience for issues covered by the media. This may cause interpersonal discussions to interact with mediated messages to produce strong agenda-setting effects.

A second factor is that issues covered in the news media may give individuals topics on which they can interpersonally communicate with others. Individuals may scan the news media for topics for discussion, then discuss them with others. Because individuals have two important sources of information on issues covered in the news media, the level of salience on these issues rises at a greater rate than the level of salience for issues not covered in the news media. For issues not covered in the news media, individuals have only limited sources of information (interpersonal communication).

Finally, interpersonal communication may lead to increased exposure to the mass media. After taking part in interpersonal discussions on issues receiving extensive coverage in the media, individuals may return to the mass media for additional information on topics that they previously discussed or plan to discuss with others in the future. In this case, interpersonal communication will lead to increased media use, which in turn leads to stronger agenda-setting effects within the individual.

Furthermore, perhaps interpersonal communication is an indication that the media messages have been received and processed by individuals. If issue information carried in media messages has not been received, the salience of issues receiving extensive coverage are identical to that of issues receiving little or no coverage. In other words, the reason individuals in some cases were not talking about issues covered in the news media is that they had not been exposed to the media. Lack of exposure transforms the mediated issues into nonmediated issues for these individuals. Regardless, the reason behind this apparent interaction should be examined in the future.

A Closer Look at Interpersonal Communication.   Although interpersonal communication clearly impacted directly on agenda-setting susceptibility here, two related variables were also examined. Included in the Jackson County study were two additional questions asking respondents about their role in the interpersonal communication and the type of discussion.

The role the respondents played was determined by responses to the following question:

> People take many different roles when talking about politics. Which of the following statements would you say best describes you when you discuss politics? Even though I may have strong opinions, I usually just listen; I listen a lot, but once in a while I express my opinions; I take an equal share in conversations; I have definite ideas and try to convince others.

The type of discussion was determined by responses to the question: "When you discuss politics, are the discussions usually: casual small-talk; in-depth discussions; or something in-between." Both of these questions were previously used in the Charlotte study (see Shaw & McCombs, 1977).

Logically, the more involved the discussion, the stronger the influence of that discussion. Thus, in-depth discussions about political issues covered in the news media should reinforce the media messages more strongly than casual small talk. If an individual takes an active role in the interpersonal communication discussions, the more likely he or she is to demonstrate agenda-setting effects. The discussions here indicate that the individuals have not only received and processed media messages, but also understood the significance well enough to feel comfortable passing on this information to others.

Pearson correlations first examined whether the respondent's role in the interpersonal communication and type of discussions were related to agenda-setting susceptibility. A regression analysis tested the relative influence of the level of interpersonal communication, the role of respondents in the discussions and the type of discussions on agenda-setting susceptibility.

As Table 4.3 shows, all three variables were strongly correlated with agenda-setting susceptibility. In other words, how often individuals discussed issues, how involved the discussions were, and how involved in the discussions the respondent was, were all positively related to agenda-setting susceptibility. In general, the higher the frequency, the higher the involvement, and the more active the role of the respondent, the stronger the agenda-setting effects.

Table 4.4 shows the regression analysis results of the three interpersonal communication variables. The frequency of communication was the strongest predictor of agenda-setting influences. In fact, frequency was so powerful that neither the type of discussion nor the role the respondent played were entered into the regression analysis after frequency was accounted for. In other words, neither the type of discussion nor the role the respondent played added significantly to the prediction of agenda-setting susceptibility after frequency was entered into the analysis. If frequency is not included in the analysis, however, both the type of discussion and the role the respondent played were powerful enough to be entered into the regression analysis.

The results here suggest that the type of discussion and the role of the respondent in the discussions may be factors in increasing issue

TABLE 4.3
Pearson Correlations Examining the Relationships Between
Interpersonal Communication Variables and Agenda-Setting Susceptibility

Variable	Pearson r	Significance
Frequency of communication	.526	.000
Intensity of discussions	.226	.000
Role of respondents	.206	.000

TABLE 4.4
Regression Analysis Results for the Influence of Interpersonal Communication Variables
on Agenda-Setting Susceptibility

Variable	Beta	Significance
Frequency of communication	.496	.001
Intensity of discussions	.065	n.s.
Role of respondents	.059	n.s.

Note. Multiple $R = .540$; R-Square $= .291$; Adjusted R-Square $= .284$.

salience. If discussions are in-depth conversations, interpersonal communication leads to higher issue salience. Thus, in-depth discussions may clear up uncertainty regarding the salience of issues better than casual small talk. Different types of interpersonal communication have different levels of impact on individuals.

The role of the respondent also plays a role in the agenda-setting process. The Pearson correlations and the second regression analysis with frequency of discussions removed both suggest that the more active the role of the respondent, the stronger the agenda-setting effects. However, neither this variable nor the type of discussion measure was strong enough to be included in the regression analysis after the frequency of discussions was accounted for. Thus, the respondent's role in the discussions, as well as the type of discussions, play a secondary role to the frequency of discussions in the agenda-setting process.

CONCLUSIONS

Overall, it appears that behavioral variables, such as interpersonal communication and media use, are important variables in the agenda-setting process. From the findings here, however, it is unclear which came first, exposure to mediated messages or interpersonal discussion of them. Perhaps some individuals use the media for information to help them in their interpersonal discussions, whereas others seek out information from the media to clear up uncertainties they experienced in their prior interpersonal discussions. An uses and gratifications approach to agenda setting and the role of interpersonal communication is an important next step in this area.

McCombs and Weaver (1985) argued for just such an examination. They argued that by merging agenda setting and uses and gratifications research, research may help develop the mass communication research field into "a more coherent paradigm" (p. 108).

Future studies in these areas seem exceptionally fruitful. As McGuire (1974) noted, utilitarian theories of media use assume that individuals are problem solvers. Individuals view the news media as valuable sources of relevant information. By seeking out information that is valuable and relevant, individuals act as active processors of information. Individuals then determine the level of influence they will be exposed to from the media. Agenda-setting effects do not passively inoculate them.

5

Putting It All Together: How the Agenda-Setting Process Works

The previous chapters have outlined some of the variables that could play important roles in the agenda-setting process. The variables have ranged from demographic to psychological to behavioral. As would be expected, some variables appeared to be closely tied to agenda setting; others were weaker factors. Still others showed no relationship with the magnitude of agenda-setting effects demonstrated by respondents.

The variables were examined in groupings based on their relatedness to each other. Thus, education and income were grouped with other demographic variables. Each set of variables, however, was examined individually. Demographic variables were isolated from psychological variables, which in turn were isolated from behavioral variables.

This chapter proposes and tests a model of agenda-setting influence based on the variables examined in the previous chapters. All three sets of variables will be time-ordered and examined together.

Obviously, variables do not act and interact in isolation. A true picture of how agenda setting works at the individual level cannot emerge from examining these variables individually. Thus, examining these groups of variables simultaneously is important in creating a better understanding of how individuals process salience cues transmitted by the news media.

THEORETICAL FRAMEWORK

Thus far, we have seen that the variables most closely related to agenda-setting susceptibility have been those factors that imply an active processing of media messages on the part of the individual. Individuals who are most likely to demonstrate strong agenda-setting effects are highly interested in political news and are high users of the news media and interpersonal communication. Thus, individuals must be motivated to seek out information about political issues and often expose themselves to issue information for the news media to have strong agenda-setting influences on them.

Active processing of information implies that individuals demonstrate agenda-setting effects based on certain personal characteristics. Highly motivated individuals with strong cognitive processing skills are most likely to display powerful agenda-setting effects. Unmotivated individuals with weak cognitive processing skills are less likely to display powerful agenda-setting influences.

The agenda-setting model proposed here examines demographics, psychographics, and behavioral variables. The model shows a logical progression based on the relative time points in which each set of variables comes into play. The variables are time-ordered so that the first variables included in the model are the variables that affect individuals earliest in their lifetime.

Therefore, the first set of variables in the model involves demographics. These variables are logically the furthest back in time from the dependent variable of agenda-setting susceptibility. The demographic variables are the first factors that affect a person's life. The demographic variables, as detailed in chapter 3, involve age, education, income, gender, and race.

The second stage of the model involves the attitudinal variables. Based on individuals' demographics, the respondents in the survey here form attitudes about both the news media and their interest in politics. These attitudinal variables are political interest and the two media credibility measures: believability and community affiliation, as detailed in chapter 3. It is assumed that demographic variables will affect an individual so that she or he can form opinions about the credibility of the media and interest levels in politics based on these factors.

The third stage involves behavioral variables. Based on their attitudes, individuals form behavioral patterns. These behavioral variables are exposure to the news media and interpersonal communication, as detailed in chapter 4. Thus, individuals' behaviors—in the form of media use and exposure to interpersonal communication—are dependent on their attitudes—credibility in the media and political interest. Individuals' attitudes, in turn, are dependent on their demographics.

Finally, the behavioral variables affect individuals. Thus, the final stage of the model deals with agenda-setting influences. Individuals' susceptibility to agenda-setting influences are dependent on their behavioral patterns—namely, how often they discuss issues with others and how often they expose themselves to the news media. As the previous stages presuppose, the behavioral patterns of individuals are dependent on their attitudes, which in turn are dependent on their demographics. Figure 5.1 details the agenda-setting model proposed here; the model argues for a linear relationship between sets of variables at each stage.

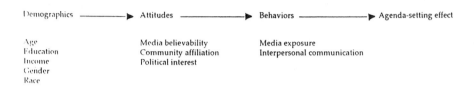

FIG. 5.1. An agenda-setting path model.

DATA ANALYSIS

To test the model, a path analysis was computed, testing the agenda-setting model in Fig. 5.1. Path analysis is a method for studying patterns of causation among a set of variables (Pedhazur, 1982). Because the agenda-setting model proposed here implies causality—exposure to the news media "causing" agenda-setting effects for individuals—using a causal modeling test such as path analysis is appropriate.

Path analysis allows for two tests. First, the path coefficients determine if the paths from one variable to another are statistically significant. In other words, path coefficients test the direction of influence from one variable to another. Statistically significant path coefficients suggest that the independent variable had a causal relationship with the dependent variable.

Path coefficients also determine the degree of influence that each of the independent variables had on the dependent variable. In other words, the path coefficients allow for the comparison of influence between the different independent variables. Larger coefficients show that one independent variable had a stronger effect on the dependent variable than a second variable that produced a smaller coefficient.

Two path models were tested here. First, because the model examined proposes a linear relationship between sets of variables, the impact of a previous group of variables was not examined in the first series of tests. That is, the impact of demographics on the psychological variables was examined. Next, the impact of the psychological variables on the behavioral variables was examined. Finally, the impact of the behavioral variables on agenda-setting susceptibility was examined. In this way, only the effects of one set of variables were examined at each stage.

The model was then re-examined, including all sets of variables previously examined. That is, the impact of demographics on the psychological variables was examined. Next, the impact of the psychological variables and demographics on the behavioral variables was examined. Finally, the impact of the behavioral variables and psychological variables and demographics on agenda-setting susceptibility was examined.

A Linear Model of Agenda Setting

Figure 5.2 gives the results of the first path analysis showing the separate stages of the path model. Several points about the model should be made.

Stage 1: Influence of Demographics on Attitudes.   The first stage of the model proposed here argues that individuals will form attitudes based on their demographics—specifically, individuals will form opinions about the news media and political interest based on their age, education, income, gender, and race. Figure 5.2 shows only the paths with statistically significant path coefficients. As this figure demonstrates, some demographic variables were more important than others in predicting individuals' attitudes.

None of the path coefficients leading from race to any of the three attitudinal variables was statistically significant. In other words, race played no role in the formation of attitudes of the respondents.

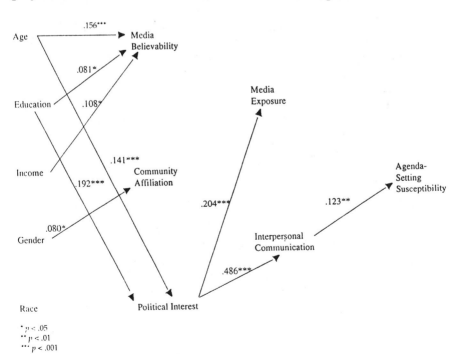

FIG. 5.2. Significant paths in the linear agenda-setting model.

Only one path coefficient from gender was statistically significant. Here, women, more than men, tended to believe the news media were looking out for the welfare of the community. Gender also was the only demographic variable to produce a statistically significant path coefficient leading to the community affiliation measure.

Age, education, and income all produced statistically significant paths leading to media believability. In general, older, highly educated individuals with high incomes were more likely to believe the news media are fair and unbiased. Age and education also produced statistically significant paths leading to political interest. Again, older, more highly educated individuals tended to show a greater interest in politics.

Overall, only certain demographics were relatively successful in predicting individuals' attitudes. Education and age were especially useful, producing statistically significant path coefficients to two of the three attitudinal variables.

Stage 2: Influence of Attitudes on Behaviors.   The second stage of the model proposed here argues that individuals form behavioral patterns based on their attitudes. In other words, individuals expose themselves to the news media and to interpersonal communication channels based on their attitudes regarding the media and political issues.

As Fig. 5.2 shows, political interest was a strong predictor of both behavioral variables. Individuals with a high interest in politics often tended to use both the news media and interpersonal communication channels.

The two media credibility measures did not produce statistically significant path coefficients to media exposure, as would seem logical. Individuals who thought the media were fair and unbiased did not tend to use the media more often than individuals who thought the media were unfair and biased. The same result was found for the perceived community affiliation measure. This supports the finding of Rimmer and Weaver (1987), who found that respondents' perceived credibility of the news media did not influence how often they used the media.

Stage 3: Influence of Behaviors on Agenda-Setting Susceptibility.   The final stage of the model argues that the behavioral patterns of individuals affect the magnitude of agenda-setting effects that these individuals demonstrate. In other words, the more exposure to the news media and the more exposure to interpersonal communication channels, the more individuals demonstrate strong agenda-setting effects.

As Fig. 5.2 shows, the path coefficient leading from interpersonal communication to agenda-setting susceptibility was statistically significant. Thus, the more interpersonal communication individuals take part in, the more susceptible they are to agenda-setting influences.

Media exposure, however, did not produce a statistically significant path coefficient. Again, this is most likely due to the power of the interpersonal communication measure. Media exposure did not add significantly to the predictability of agenda-setting susceptibility when the influence of interpersonal communication had been accounted for. As a result, the path model proposed here needs several modifications.

Race was completely ineffective in the model, producing no statistically significant path coefficients. Gender was somewhat ineffective in the model, producing one significant path coefficient—to perceived community affiliation of the media. It also should be noted that because community affiliation did not lead to either media exposure or interpersonal communication, this also demonstrates a lack of power for the gender variable in the agenda-setting process.

Thus, the most effective demographics involved the variables that were most closely associated with highly active information processors. Education and age appeared to be the most powerful demographics. These variables directly affected both the respondents' perceived believability in the news media and their interest in politics. Younger individuals with low education were more likely to be uninterested in politics and to feel the media are biased and unfair.

Of the psychological variables, political interest was clearly the most powerful, producing statistically significant path coefficients to both of the behavioral variables. Political interest was positively related to both media exposure and exposure to interpersonal communication. Perceived believability in the media and perceived community affiliation of the media did not produce any statistically significant path coefficients.

Again, this offers some support for the notion of active processing of information in the agenda-setting process. The individuals most likely to expose themselves to the media and to interpersonal communication channels are those individuals who are highly interested in politics. Those individuals with low interest in politics are less likely to use the news media or to discuss issues with others. Thus, uninterested individuals are highly inactive information seekers.

Of the behavior variables, only interpersonal communication produced a statistically significant path coefficient to the agenda-setting susceptibility measure. As mentioned in chapter 4, there are several possibilities for the finding that interpersonal communication is more powerful than media exposure for predicting agenda-setting susceptibility. Interpersonal communication reinforces media messages by giving individuals a second exposure to information on important issues. It also may be an indication that media messages were received by individuals. Individuals talk about important issues because they saw the issues in the news media. Media exposure may also be a relatively stable behavior across all individuals. Thus, media exposure may have shown less variance than interpersonal communication, which may have suppressed the path coefficients found here.

Regardless of the reason, the finding suggests that the individuals most susceptible to agenda-setting effects are active processors. People who talk a lot about issues show the strongest agenda-setting effects. People who do not discuss issues with others are less likely to demonstrate strong agenda-setting effects.

The Full Model of Agenda Setting

Figure 5.3 shows the results of full agenda-setting model when all previous variables are included in subsequent stages. A number of other significant paths were found here.

In Stage 2, besides political interest impacting on media exposure, three paths leading from demographic variables were statistically significant. Age, education, and income all led to media exposure. As many previous studies have found (see Stone, 1987), older, highly educated individuals with higher incomes reported using the news media more than younger, lower educated individuals with low incomes.

Two additional paths were statistically significant leading to interpersonal communication. Here, education and income both led to interpersonal communication. Higher educated individuals with

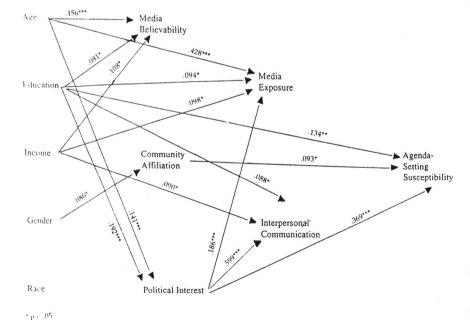

FIG. 5.3. All significant paths in the agenda-setting model.

higher incomes tended to be more likely to take part in interpersonal discussions.

Finally, three additional paths leading to agenda-setting susceptibility were statistically significant. These involved political interest, community affiliation, and education. Highly educated individuals, who believed the news media watch out for the community's welfare and who are highly interested in politics, were more likely to show a stronger susceptibility to agenda-setting influences.

It should be noted that when education, political interest, and community affiliation were accounted for, interpersonal communication was no longer a significant predictor of agenda-setting susceptibility. Thus, education, community affiliation, and political interest were all stronger predictors of agenda-setting susceptibility than was interpersonal communication.

CONCLUSIONS

Overall, three of the five demographic variables included in this study were relatively useful in predicting both attitudes and behaviors of individuals. The exceptions were gender and race. Only for gender, in the case of the attitudinal variable of perceived community affiliation of the news media, did either of the two variables demonstrate an influence. Thus, gender and race appeared to play an extremely limited role in the agenda-setting process.

Education, age, and income, on the other hand, produced several significant path coefficients. Education was especially influential, affecting respondents' attitudes on the perceived believability of the news media, their interest in politics, their level of interpersonal communication, their exposure to news media, and, finally, their susceptibility to agenda-setting influences. Age, although not impacting directly on agenda-setting susceptibility as education did, nonetheless, did influence respondents' perceived believability of the media, their interest in politics, and their exposure to the news media. Income affected respondents' believability in the news media, their exposure to the news media, and their level of interpersonal communication.

Behavioral variables produced mixed results. Interpersonal communication produced a significant path coefficient in the linear model of agenda setting, but this relationship disappeared when other factors—psychological and demographic variables—were taken into account. Thus, the demographic variable of education and the attitudinal variables of political interest and perceived community affiliation of the media were stronger predictors of agenda-setting susceptibility than was the frequency of interpersonal communication.

Media exposure demonstrated no relationship to agenda-setting susceptibility in either the linear path model or the full path model.

Variables other than media exposure were more powerful in predicting agenda-setting susceptibility. This is not to argue that exposure to the news media is unrelated to agenda-setting. As the Pearson correlations in chapter 4 demonstrate, the higher the exposure level to the news media, the stronger the agenda-setting effect. There was a positive relationship between exposure to media messages and the effect of these messages on individuals, but the linkage between exposure and effect is weak when compared to other variables, such as interpersonal communication. Exposure was especially deferential to the psychological variable of political interest.

The strongest influence in the full model was a psychological variable—political interest. Again, this suggests that agenda setting is a highly active process. If individuals are highly interested in politics, they are most likely to show strong agenda-setting effects. Thus, uninterested individuals do not show strong agenda-setting effects. Individuals must display a strong motivational need for information contained in the news media for the messages contained in the media to have a strong influence. This motivational need was demonstrated here through the powerful influence of political interest on agenda-setting susceptibility.

Perceived community affiliation of the media also had an influence on agenda-setting susceptibility. Two explanations for this significant path coefficient are plausible. First, a reverse causal relationship may exist. That is, perhaps agenda-setting susceptibility leads to high perceived community affiliation. In other words, individuals who display strong agenda-setting effects tend to believe the news media are looking out for their community's welfare because they agree with the media coverage. Individuals may become influenced by media coverage of issues and then believe the media are looking out for the community's welfare. In this case, agenda-setting influences precede the perceived community affiliation of the news media.

Second, perhaps the perceived community affiliation leads directly to agenda-setting susceptibility regardless of media exposure. In other words, if individuals believe the news media are looking out for the community's welfare, exposure does not matter. The individuals believe the issues covered in the media are important regardless of if they are high media users or low media users. Behavioral variables are not important. Indeed, community affiliation did not lead to media exposure. Thus, exposure is not a necessary condition, intervening between high perceived community affiliation and high agenda-setting effects.

A final point should be made about the role of education in the agenda-setting process. According to the full model of agenda setting, education directly affected agenda-setting susceptibility. Again, highly educated individuals were most likely to demonstrate strong agenda-setting effects. Highly educated individuals understand the significance of coverage in the news media, and thus are more susceptible to influences due to coverage of issues in the media. Low-educated individuals are less efficient in understanding the significance of issue coverage, and thus are less likely to show strong agenda-setting effects.

If agenda setting is actually "social learning," then it is apparent from the results here that the most efficient learners are those individuals who are highly educated and who are highly motivated to learn information about important issues because of a high interest in politics. Thus, attitudinal motivations, such as interest in politics, and the ability to understand the significance of media coverage are the keys to the agenda-setting process.

MEDIA RELIANCE AS AN ADDITIONAL VARIABLE

Because the two attitudinal variables dealing with the perceived credibility of the media seem to have limited influence on the behavioral variables and the agenda-setting susceptibility measure, an additional analysis was conducted. Perhaps credibility does not lead directly to exposure to the media, but instead leads indirectly to media exposure through a second attitudinal variable—namely, media reliance.

A media reliance measure was included in the initial Jackson County, Illinois survey. The measure involved two items that asked respondents if they strongly agreed, agreed, were neutral, disagreed, or strongly disagreed with the following statements: "I rely on the stories in the newspaper for information about politics and important issues;" and "I rely on TV news for information about politics and important issues." Responses to these items were summed, then used in an additional path model. The variable was placed after the media credibility measure and before the media exposure measure. Thus, the new path model proposed that demographics lead to perceived credibility, which in turn leads to media reliance, which leads to exposure to the media, which ultimately leads to agenda-setting susceptibility.

As with perceptions of the credibility of the media, individuals also rely on the news media for information to varying degrees. However, if individuals perceive the media to be highly credible, they may also rely heavily on the media for information about events and news topics.

DeFleur and Ball-Rokeach (1989) noted that individuals develop dependencies on the mass media because people tend to be goal-oriented and often require resources controlled by the media to achieve their goals. If individuals have a goal of gaining information on the important issues of the day, they will become highly dependent on the media because the media control access to a variety of information.

This media system dependency theory closely matches *the need for orientation concept* (see Weaver, 1977). This concept posits that if an issue is highly relevant to an individual, and the individual has a high degree of uncertainty about the issue, he or she will be highly susceptible to media agendasetting effects. Therefore, according to both the media system dependency theory and the need for orientation concept, high reliance on the mass media leads to high agenda-setting effects.

Though research into media reliance has been extensive (e.g., Ball-Rokeach, Rokeach, & Grube, 1984; Becker, Sobowale, & Cobbey, 1979; Becker & Whitney, 1980; McDonald, 1990; McLeod & McDonald, 1985), few scholars have attempted to tie reliance to agenda-setting effects. One such study (Erbring et al., 1980) found that agenda-setting effects were most pronounced for individuals who were highly dependent on the news media for information.

The question of which comes first in this process—credibility or reliance—however, is unclear. DeFleur and Ball-Rokeach (1989) suggested that individuals develop reliance on a media system first. They then develop "affective arousal"—that is, likes and dislikes—toward the system. They hypothesized that the greater the intensity of dependencies, the greater the degree of affective arousal. In other words, if individuals are strongly dependent on a medium, they will soon develop strong likes or dislikes—possibly developing opinions as to the credibility of the medium. According to this scenario, reliance leads to credibility.

However, McLeod and McDonald (1985) suggested the opposite could be true. In their regression analysis of media orientations, they found that reliance on a medium was a poor predictor of effects. They suggested that this lack of power could be due to antecedents of reliance. One potential antecedent variable could be credibility. The new model proposed here follows this rationale. Thus, media reliance is placed after perceived credibility.

The results of the secondary analysis are shown in Fig. 5.4. As the figure demonstrates, the new path model works exceptionally well. Examining only the Jackson County data, then, the path coefficients from the two credibility indexes to the exposure measure, again, were not statistically significant. This supports the finding of Rimmer and Weaver (1987), who found that media credibility did not correlate with frequency of use.

However, the path coefficients from the believability index (.182), from the affiliation index (.249), and from political interest (.103) to the reliance measure were all statistically significant. In addition, the path coefficients from the reliance measure to the exposure measure (.253) and from the exposure measure to the agenda-setting susceptibility index (.109) were also significant. Thus, the data here offer strong support for a linear model of agenda setting—if reliance is included in the analysis. Demographics lead to attitudes toward the media, which in turn leads to reliance on the media, followed by exposure to the media and ultimately agenda-setting effects. Additional analyses examined newspapers and television separately. In both cases, the path coefficient trends were identical.

Overall, the findings suggest that the original agenda-setting model needs to be modified. As the secondary analysis shows, media reliance may be an important intervening variable in the relationship between media credibility and media exposure.

The secondary analysis also suggests that media believability may play a more important role in the agenda-setting process than the initial path analysis showed, though that role is as an indirect influence on agenda-setting susceptibility. In other words, although believability did not lead directly to media exposure or to agenda-setting susceptibility, it did lead indirectly to agenda setting by influencing individuals' levels of reliance on the news media. Reliance, in turn, led to exposure, which then led to agenda-setting effects.

Clearly, then, the inclusion of media reliance in the agenda-setting model improves the fit with the data. Thus, an important second psychological stage—that of the formation of a dependency on the media for information—was missing from the initial model. The modified model, then, has four stages.

In the first stage of the modified agenda-setting model, individuals form opinions based on their demographics. Older, more highly educated

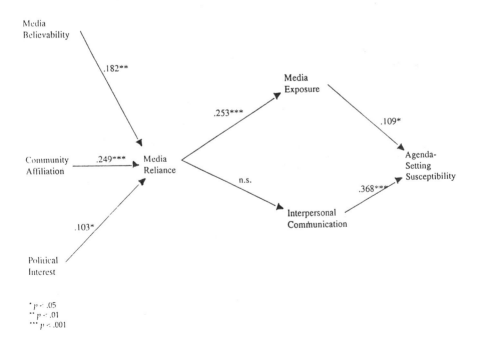

FIG. 5.4. Role of reliance in the agenda-setting model, using Jackson County data only.

individuals tend to believe the media are doing a good job of providing fair news coverage and tend to be highly interested in politics.

In the second stage of the agenda-setting model, individuals form a dependency on the news media for information based on their perceptions regarding the credibility of the media. Individuals who believe the media are highly credible become highly reliant on them for information.

In the third stage of the model, individuals expose themselves to the media based on their level of reliance on the media. Individuals who are highly reliant on the news media for information often expose themselves to the news media. Individuals highly reliant on the news media also tend to use interpersonal communication channels often.

In the final stage of the model, individuals demonstrate agenda-setting effects based on their exposure to the news media and level of interpersonal communication in which they take part. Individuals who often use the media and who often discuss issues with others are highly susceptible to agenda-setting effects. Additional analyses show that this pattern holds for newspapers, television, and the two media combined.

Several other variables outside the linear model also should be noted. Only one demographic variable—age—led directly to media reliance ($\beta = .167; p = .002$). Older individuals were more reliant on the news media for information than younger individuals.

Age ($\beta = .247; p = .000$) and education ($\beta = .145; p = .007$) also produced significant path coefficients leading to media use. Again, older, highly educated individuals use the media more, as several previous studies have noted. These paths also were significant in the original model examined here.

Finally, as with the initial full model of agenda setting examined here, both political interest ($\beta = .182; p = .001$) and the perceived community affiliation of the news media ($\beta = .198; p = .001$) produced statistically significant path coefficients leading directly to agenda-setting susceptibility.

Reliance, however, did not produce a statistically significant path coefficient leading to interpersonal communication. This finding on the surface seems logical. Respondents' professed reliance on the media for information should not lead to increased use of interpersonal communication channels. These two variables appeared to be conceptually unrelated.

However, as with the full model, political interest ($\beta = .312; p = .000$) was strongly related to interpersonal communication frequency. Education ($\beta = .113; p = .049$) also produced a significant path coefficient with interpersonal communication.

Overall, the inclusion of media reliance served mainly as a psychological linkage between respondents' attitudes toward the media and their levels of exposure. Individuals did not change their media use behavior based on their attitudes toward the media. Individuals first formed a level of reliance on the media based on their perceptions of the credibility of the media. People who believed the media are believable and looking out for the community's welfare formed strong reliance on the media for information. Only after forming a psychological reliance on the media for information did individuals then decide on their level of exposure to media messages. The level of reliance, then, is a critical stage in the agenda-setting process.

6

Effects of Different Media on Agenda Setting

Agenda setting affects different individuals to differing degrees. As previous chapters demonstrated, highly educated, highly motivated individuals are most susceptible to agenda-setting effects.

It stands to reason, then, that different media affect individuals to differing degrees as well. A visual medium, such as television, should involve a different type of information processing in an individual than a textual medium, such as newspapers.

The mental processing of information obtained through the mass media is extremely complex. Individuals attend to, process, and retain a wide variety of information in many different ways.

Of concern here is how this mental processing differs between broadcast and print media. Several scholars have noted differences between media. In his controversial book *Understanding Media*, McLuhan argued that each medium has fundamental and unique characteristics. The information distributed by the media was much less important compared to the medium itself. McLuhan (1964) argued that "the personal and social consequences of any medium—that is, of any extension of ourselves—result from the new scale that is introduced into our affairs by each extension of ourselves, or by any new technology" (p. 7).

The technical aspects of mass communication deserve further attention from researchers, especially in light of the current explosion of new technologies in mass communication. The medium, although it may not be the message in and of itself, certainly plays a role in the mental processing of information that it delivers.

Scholars have long argued that the mental processing of information varies for different media. Obviously, reading newspapers is a very different cognitive task than viewing television. Two basic arguments have been proposed regarding information processing differences across media. These arguments are based on medium characteristics and receiver characteristics (or the mental effort involved in processing messages).

MEDIUM CHARACTERISTICS

More than three decades ago, McLuhan (1964) categorized media based on the involvement each demanded from individuals. Television and newspapers were at opposite ends of his continuum. McLuhan called newspapers "hot" because they provided a great deal of detail and left the reader with little to add from her or his own experiences or knowledge. According to him, a hot medium extended a single sense in "high definition," but required the receiver to have low involvement with the message. Television, however, was a "cool" medium because it provided little detail, but extended several senses. A cool medium requires the receiver of messages to have high involvement with the message.

Although McLuhan met with widespread criticism, some of his ideas, at least on the surface, appear pertinent even today. Contrary to McLuhan's argument, whereas the different media may not be more important than the messages they convey, newspapers, magazines, television, and radio, nonetheless, differ from each other, with each having its own strengths and weaknesses. Moreover, individuals process information from each differently. If individuals process information obtained from various media differently, the effects of the information will logically differ. According to McLuhan, television, as a cool medium, requires more "physical filling in" by the audience than a hot medium such as newspapers. Television requires more concentration than mere looking because the dots of the screen only offer outlines of figures. Viewers must learn to fill in the characters on the screen—in a sort of Gestalt process—to complete the communication process. Thus, television viewers must have high involvement with the televised message.

If this is true, the overall impact of television on individuals should logically be stronger. With more types of information impacting on a viewer, television inundates individuals with visual and verbal information. The individual, however, has to actively sort through the information and connect it all together. McLuhan said that TV engages viewers. Television viewers must actively fill in details around televised information.

On the other hand, the more detailed newspaper accounts require less involvement from the reader. According to McLuhan, there is less "filling in" for readers to do because newspaper accounts address fewer senses. Singer (1980) took exactly the opposite stand in McLuhan's involvement argument. He argued that because humans are active processors of information, they make use of schemata, memory, and imagination when deciding which information should be used and which information should be screened out, as well as how to organize this information.

Readers are able to take full advantage of their cognitive potential with newspapers because of the characteristics of the print media. The rapid pacing of television makes the use of schemata, memory, and imagination more difficult. Thus, readers always process information more thoughtfully and more thoroughly than do television viewers.

In addition, the amount of information presented on television can tax processing capacity, so much so that viewers may not pick up important information—especially when the content of the program is complex. Pacing is out of the viewer's control, meaning that information stimuli from television are seen as a blur because viewers cannot discriminate between sights and sounds. In fact, pacing is so rapid that the viewer is unable to do extensive processing of incoming information.

Information is presented so quickly that viewers find it extremely difficult to integrate television content with information already stored in their memories. Thus, cognitive operations are hampered, which leads to greater difficulty when a person attempts to retrieve information from her or his memory.

In short, Singer (1980) argued that this superficial processing of televised information leads to stronger recognition but poorer recall of memory. Stronger agenda-setting effects for newspapers, then, are expected. If people can recall information from newspapers better than from television, individuals would be able to recall salience cues better from newspapers—especially over long periods of time when memory decay might set in.

In sharp contrast is the mental processing involved in reading of newspapers. Reading allows for more focused concentration because printed words are isolated from other distractions, such as moving images and sounds. More complicated cognitive operations occur in reading. A reader must first read and translate words, while also using his or her imagination to "see and hear" action described in the text. Singer (1980) argued that reading "requires us to draw upon our own memories and fantasies, to take the time to try to follow the drift of the writer and to conjure up by ourselves exotic settings, sights and sounds suggested in the text" (p.48). This complex cognitive processing does not occur with television because of the addition of audio and visual information. These additional stimuli provide viewers with "an external image that one can passively lean on, rather than forming one's own" (p. 57).

The advantages of print media are especially apparent when complex material is presented. The printed word helps provide readers with "logical direction to thought " (Singer, 1980, p. 59). Reading, then, is a superior medium for enhancing recall.

Krugman argued for a more active processing for print media as well. In a series of experiments examining how individuals learn from advertisements, Krugman (1965, 1966, 1970) found that individuals have low involvement with broadcast messages. He also found that involvement with advertising was actually higher for magazines than for television.

Individuals still learned some information from television commercials, but this learning was passive and "characterized by an absence of resistance to what is learned" (Krugman & Hartley, 1970, p. 184).

MENTAL EFFORT DIFFERENCES

The basis for the mental effort argument is quite simple: The amount of information people learn from individual media is dependent, to a large degree, on the amount of effort they must put forth in processing this information. Thus, the greater the effort individuals put forth, the more information they gain.

Logically, newspaper reading takes a great deal more effort than television viewing because reading is a more difficult task than television viewing. Individuals cannot passively watch as someone else reads them the news. Newspaper readers must actively determine which newspapers stories they will read and which stories they will not read. Thus, individuals should learn more from newspaper reading than from television viewing.

Salomon (1979) is one of the chief proponents of this argument. He argued that expections play a role in information processing. People *expect* reading will be more difficult. Preconceived notions about the amount of mental effort, therefore, come into play. Readers expect reading to be more difficult, so they put more effort into reading than television viewers put into viewing television. Therefore, learning is enhanced by reading. Individuals learn less from viewing because they expect to expend little effort when watching television.

According to Salomon (1979), this expected mental effort influences how individuals process information. People allocate more mental effort to reading than to watching television. Memory of content is therefore often superior in reading compared to television viewing. Salomon further argued that the amount of mental effort allocated to a task is a function of perceived-task difficulty. Preconceptions about the relative difficulty involved in processing information from print and/or television forces the receiver to allocate more mental effort to a printed message than to a televised message.

Applying Salomon's arguments to agenda setting, we expect to find stronger agenda-setting effects for newspapers than for television. Because agenda setting is a form of social learning, individuals should learn more information about the relative importance of issues through newspapers than through television news.

Differences in Processing Print and Broadcast Messages

Several differences between television news and newspapers affect how individuals process information transmitted by the two media. Television news has an advantage in that it is more visually oriented and employs more types of information (i.e., sight, sound, and motion) than newspapers. However, newspapers have an advantage in that individuals can process information contained in them when it is most convenient for the reader and at a pace that is best suited for the reader. Both of these factors are important.

Broadcast Advantages. Previous research suggests that visual information is more easily processed than verbal information. Son, Reese, and Davie (1987), for example, found that visuals can improve recall of television news stories. Culbertson (1974) found that photographs were rated more emotional than verbal descriptions, indicating that visual information may have a more powerful emotional impact on individuals than the written word. The physiology of the processing of visual information offers one clue why visual information has such a strong effect on individuals.

Lester (1995) provided an excellent explanation of the physiological effects of visual information on individuals. Several points are especially pertinent. Processing visual information involves several stages. Visual information processing begins as light that the eye sees. The light is then processed by the eye's retina, a net of about 125 million light receptors lining about 85% of the back of the eye. Before light reaches the net of photoreceptors at the retina, it goes through several areas of the eye: the cornea, the liquid aqueous, the iris, the lens, the vitreous humor, and small blood vessels.

The retina contains two types of photoreceptors: rods and cones. The 118 million rods, long and slender in shape, are primarily responsible for night vision. The 7 million cones, shaped like upside-down funnels, allow individuals to see colors. The electrical energy of light is converted by the rods and cones into the chemical energy that the brain can use. The rods and cones provide a pathway to a series of neuron connections leading to the optic nerve. The optic nerves from each eye intersect behind the eyeballs at the optic chasm.

Finally, after passing through the eye, retina, and optic nerve, light reaches the brain. The entire trip from the retina to the brain takes about three thousandths of a second. The optic nerves make a connection to the part of the brain called the *thalamus*, which receives the impulses from the optic nerve and transfers them to the visual cortex located in the back of the cerebrum. Only about 10% of the visual cortex is actually used for processing visual information. Visual messages can be identified in the visual cortex, but the visual image is stored in the *hippocampus*, a memory storage area in which new images are compared with old pictures already stored.

Physiology points to several factors that influence the processing of visual information. The brain cells in the visual cortex respond to four elements: color, form, depth, and movement. Television utilizes three of these elements: color, form, and movement; newspapers utilize two: color and form. Thus, adding the third element of movement to information further stimulates the visual cortex, which may, in turn, increase the overall effect of the information.

Television also utilizes the additional element of sound. By employing sound, visuals, and motion, television provides viewers with a greater variety of information than newspapers. Because television has more types of information to process than newspapers, information from newscasts may have a more powerful agenda-setting effect on their viewers than newspapers have on their readers.

Print Advantages. Newspapers could have a stronger agenda-setting effect than television for several reasons. Whereas television inundates viewers with several types of information, newspapers, nonetheless, offer one significant advantage over the broadcast media: Newspapers are a more permanent source of information. Although television offers viewers sight, sound, and motion, newspapers provide readers with a source of news that is readily available for use at any time of day. The permanency of newspapers is important for two reasons.

First, readers can process information contained in newspapers at their own pace. Unless viewers tape news broadcasts, they must watch and process the evening news while it is being broadcast. If a news segment is paced too quickly, a viewer may not have time to process the information contained within it. Meanwhile, a reader can read a story, stop, contemplate the significance, and return to the story for additional information. If readers want to stop and contemplate the significance of a story, they can do so at as leisurely a pace as they see fit.

Second, readers can return to newspapers at more than one point in time. Viewers must watch and process information from the evening news only while it is being broadcast. If a viewer is distracted, even for just a moment, the viewer cannot return to the broadcast at a later time to review the story. The missed segment is gone forever. Readers, however, can skip stories or even entire sections and return to them whenever they want. These two factors are important advantages in the agenda-setting process.

Newspaper research suggests that readers read the newspaper whenever it is convenient for them—at various times during the day. Because readers read the news when they want to and at the pace they want to, the information contained in the newspaper may have a more powerful effect than television news.

Television research, however, suggests that, although viewers now have more potential news sources than ever before (CNN, Headline News), most continue to view the evening news at traditional times. Viewers demonstrate little control over when they watch the news or how the news is paced. Broadcast news, therefore, may have less of an effect on individuals than the print media.

Differences in News Presentation

In addition to the type of processing involved by print and broadcast news consumers, the nature of the news in the two media also differs. The presentation styles of stories reported in newspapers and on network news are vastly different.

McClure and Patterson (1976) noted that newspapers have several advantages over television news. They can clearly demonstrate the significance they attach to a given story through traditional means of indicating emphasis and significance. These significance cues include whether a story is long or short, whether it has an accompanying picture or no accompanying picture, whether it has a large headline or a small headline, whether the story is on the front page or a back page, and whether it is run above the fold or below the fold. The print medium, in other words, gives readers a strong, lasting visual indication of the news.

Television news, McClure and Patterson (1976) argued, gives limited coverage to a large number of stories, rather than providing in-depth reports, as newspapers do. Newscasts provide "little hard issue content, little information about the positions of candidates and almost no background or contextual information to give the voter perspective" (pp. 25–26).

The lead story on a network news broadcast gives a strong indication to viewers that the issue covered in the story is important. Yet the rapid pace of the telecast can confuse viewers beyond the lead story. In other words, they may have a difficult time differentiating between stories beyond the lead story. Is the second story, which is only 20 seconds long, more important than the third story, which is 2 minutes long? From a news director's standpoint, the answer is yes, but the evidence from a news consumer's standpoint is less clear.

Moreover, what about the closing story, which often involves an in-depth analysis that might last 4 or 5 minutes? A news consumer would likely believe that an issue addressed in such a fashion must be highly important, yet because the story is at the end of the newscasts, some viewers may consider it to be of minimal importance.

McClure and Patterson (1976) noted that television, despite its shortcomings, has a strong impact in some instances. They argued that if television news breaks into regular entertainment programming, this break in routine greatly affects viewers. Nonetheless, television is dependent on exciting and directly relevant visual presentations. McCombs (1977) similarly argued that the medium shapes the message. He noted that newspapers utilize dozens of pages and thus, pick up public issues earlier in their life cycle.

Because they can track public issues earlier, newspapers often take the lead in presenting issues to the public.

AGENDA SETTING AND THE DIFFERENT MEDIA

Of concern here, then, is how the rise and fall of the coverage of issues on the mass media agenda is related to the public agenda. Three differences in effects across the media are examined. First is the magnitude of effect. From the previous discussion, a strong case can be made for both television and newspapers having a stronger agenda-setting influence on individuals than the other type of medium.

Second is the optimal time lag for agenda-setting effects to occur. Several previous studies (Stone & McCombs, 1981; Winter & Eyal, 1981; Zucker, 1978) addressed this issue. None of these studies, however, attempted to examine differences in time lag for different mass media simultaneously.

Third is the decay of the agenda-setting effect. Given the fact that individuals have a limited ability to retain information, it is likely that agenda-setting effects decay differently for issue information presented in the print and broadcast media. Obviously, individuals do not remember everything they read in the newspaper or everything they view on television, especially as new information becomes available to replace old information. In other words, an individual's memory of information gained from the news media decays over time.

THEORETICAL FRAMEWORK

One of the most important considerations that agenda-setting researchers must address is what time frame they employ in their analyses. In other words, researchers must decide how far back in time they will go to analyze media content prior to their field work. As Winter and Eyal (1981) noted, "Since most of these studies measure and compare the media and public agendas over time, the temporal variable would appear to be crucial" (p. 376).

Time-lag selection is especially important in agenda-setting research because studies in this area investigate a causal hypothesis. Chaffee (1972) argued that a time lag that is too short does not capture the causal relationship, but a time lag that is too long is also a serious problem because "there is always the danger that a causal effect will 'dissipate' over time if the researcher waits too long to measure it."

Salwen (1988) believed the time-lag question to be important because researchers need to confine their measures of media coverage to as short a time period as possible because "any time discrepancies in the measurement of the public agenda may affect the public's evaluations of issue salience" (p.101).

Despite the importance of a precise time frame, many discrepancies remain regarding the optimal time period to include in agenda-setting studies. Studies have examined issues in time frames as short as 1 week (Becker & McCombs, 1977; Mullins, 1977), and as long as 9 months (Sohn, 1978). Funkhouser (1973) compared media coverage across a decade with public concern in the same time period. Furthermore, even the few studies that have dealt specifically with the time-lag question have produced inconsistent results. The optimal time lags for these studies varied from a 4-month period stretching from 2 to 6 months before the survey period (Stone & McCombs, 1981) to 0 to 2 weeks before the survey period (Eaton, 1989).

The varied results on the optimal agenda-setting time lag, however, could be due to methodologies employed. Stone and McCombs (1981) examined two news magazines: *Time* and *Newsweek*. Eaton (1989) examined complete agendas based on biweekly data collected from three network broadcasts, four newspapers, and three newsmagazines combined.

Other studies examining time-lag differences also used a variety of methods. Winter and Eyal (1981) studied one issue (civil rights) from 1954 to 1976 and front-page coverage in *The New York Times*. Salwen (1988) also looked at one issue (the environment) and its coverage in the three largest daily newspapers serving Lansing, Michigan. Zucker (1978) investigated four issues across time and coverage on the three national networks.

In addition, most of the research dealing with the time-lag question examined one issue, or a series of single issues, across time. Yet, given the large number of *Type I studies* (McCombs, 1981)—which examine an entire agenda of issues covered by the news media and an entire agenda of issues perceived as important by members of the public—an investigation comparing complete media and public agendas is sorely needed. This type of examination allows for an investigation of the interrelatedness of issues, an important consideration given the recent research that suggests issues compete with each other in a "zero-sum" game (Zhu, 1992).

Previous research has also noted the possibility of differences between the news media. Several researchers (McClure & Patterson, 1976; Tipton, Haney, & Basehart, 1975) found that newspapers correlate better than television with voter agendas. Shaw and McCombs (1977) argued that television news might have a stronger short-term impact, but newspaper content may have a more consistent effect across longer periods of time. Zucker (1978), on the other hand, argued that at the national level, the public may be more influenced by the three networks' newscasts than by newspapers because of television's accessibility.

A number of researchers have also suggested that national news media, to a large degree, set the agenda of issues covered by local media. Breed (1955), for example, suggested that news flows downward from the elite dailies. In other words, small dailies learn coverage patterns from larger newspapers. Crouse (1972) similarly argued that the elite media, such as *The New York Times*, influence the national agenda. Front-page coverage in *The New York Times*, he concluded, means prominent coverage in every other paper in America.

Thus, if smaller, more localized media react to the national media, the national media may have a more immediate effect on the public. In other words, if local media follow national media coverage, issues in the local press take longer to reach the general public than ones in the national or regional media—and consequently, take longer to influence the public agenda. However, because the national media may first influence local media and then the public, the national media may show a slower decay in effect over time.

In addition, national media also devote more coverage to international and national issues than do local media. Indeed, the traditional agenda-setting question, which was employed here, asks respondents, "What is the number one problem facing our *country* today?" Given that this question addresses a national agenda, national media should have a stronger agenda-setting effect than local media, which must devote significant coverage to issues of local concern. As a result, individuals may demonstrate a slower memory decay for national issues covered by the national media.

Added to the mix of factors surrounding the time-lag question is the role of memory decay. Individuals do not remember equally as well media content across several days. Thus, the time period when agenda-setting effects disappear is as important to researchers as a precise optimal time lag. In other words, at what point do individuals fail to recall the issue information transmitted by the news media and accumulated in media consumers' memories?

The study of memory and its decay dates back to before the turn of the century. In a series of experiments conducted by Ebbinghaus (1885), lists of words were learned and relearned on successive days. The amounts of time necessary for successful learning each day were noted and later compared to each other in order to discuss the relationship between information retention and time. From the resulting graph, Ebbinghaus—and subsequent researchers who further upheld his findings—concluded that the "main characteristic [of human memory decay] is a rapid fall immediately after learning and a gradual flattening out as the interval is prolonged. Forgetting becomes more and more gradual as time advances " (Woodworth & Schlosberg, 1954, p. 726). Furthermore, when Ebbinghaus plotted his data against the logarithm of time, he observed that "retention declines approximately in proportion to the log of time" (p. 726).

Watt, Mazza, and Snyder (1993) used this exponential expression of memory decay over time when analyzing three issues presented in television newscasts and their agenda-setting effects. In order to account for past coverage of an issue in addition to current stories, Watt et al. modified the Ebbinghaus curve. The resulting formula analyzed memory decay of all issue coverage and its effect on audience issue salience, while also accounting for issue prominence (i.e., where it was placed within the newscasts) and issue obtrusiveness (i.e., personal experience with an issue by audience members).

In addition to altering the Ebbinghaus curve, Watt et al. used the concept of a "time window" to account for past, accumulated coverage and current news stories about an issue. These time windows, or data sampling periods of variable length, are used to determine "how long...people continue to be affected by past stories in the media " (Watt et al., 1993, p. 409). As with Ebbinghaus' memory loss hypothesis, all issue coverage and salience in the time window should proportionately decay. Given the mathematical fact that an exponential decay never reaches zero, Watt et al. assumed an eventual memory loss of 95% as the maximum loss of story impact in each time window. Their results show that different issues show their strongest agenda-setting correlations when analyzed within different time windows. Their memory decay time windows ranged from 12 to 60 days for Iran to 600 days for inflation.

This analysis builds on the groundwork laid by Watt et al. (1993). Instead of examining individual issues in time windows of up to 2 years, however, this chapter investigates three different news media for shorter time frames. Logically, a news report should not have an influence on individuals 600 days later—as found by Watt et al. This analysis examines daily coverage for 6 months for two news media and for 50 days for a third.

DATA ANALYSIS

The data analysis involved only the survey of the Eugene–Springfield area. The public agenda was determined by responses to the traditional agenda-setting question: "What is the number one problem facing our country today?" This question was asked of respondents before the agenda-setting susceptibility measures were given so that the issue categories utilized in the previous sections of the book did not give respondents ideas about issues they could report.

The 12 issues that were mentioned most often by respondents were included in the study. The percentage of respondents that mentioned each issue as being the most important problem determined where the issues ranked on the public agenda. Coverage of the 12 issues were then examined in three news media: the national broadcasts of ABC World News Tonight, the local broadcasts of the evening news for the station with the highest ratings in the area surveyed, and a local morning daily newspaper serving the area. The ABC broadcasts were coded through the Vanderbilt Television News Abstracts for the 6 months preceding the first day of our survey. In a few cases, always on either a Saturday or Sunday, ABC did not have a national broadcast. To maintain consistent time intervals, a broadcast of either CBS or NBC was coded on these days.

The local television broadcasts were coded through station logs for the 50 days preceding the first day of the survey. Only 50 days of logs were available for this study. Finally, the front pages of the main news section were coded for the local daily newspaper for the 6 months preceding the first day of our survey. Intercoder reliability using Scott's pi averaged .89.

Each news story was weighted according to the distance in time from the date of broadcast to the start of the survey period. The weights were determined by the memory decay curve proposed by Ebbinghaus (1885, for a more detailed description of the memory curve developed by Ebbinghaus, see Woodworth & Schlosberg, 1954).The weights are based on two main assumptions:

1. Individuals eventually retain only about 5% of all knowledge that they learn. In other words, 95% of an individual's memory decays.
2. Memory decay is not linear. That is, memory decays rapidly at first, then slows.

The effects of the accumulated weighted coverage were then examined for each day of the study. For example, for Day 1, the day before the beginning of the survey period, the coverage of issues televised on that day was weighted by .05, again, under the assumption that memory decays 95%. For Day 2, the coverage of the day before the survey was weighted by .10 and coverage of 2 days before the survey was weighted by .05. These weighted scores were then summed. For Day 3, weights ranged from .12 to .08 to .05. Each subsequent day was weighted similarly, so that coverage the farthest from the survey period was weighted by .05 and the other dates were weighted based on the Ebbinghaus curve—a rapid drop off immediately followed by a slower decline.

Thus, the coverage closest to our survey period received a heavier weight than coverage farther back in time. Indeed, if Ebbinghaus' memory decay curve is correct, information gained recently should be recalled more efficiently than older information and thus should have a stronger agenda-setting effect on individuals.

Spearman rank-order correlations were then computed examining the relationships between the accumulated weighted coverage of the 12 issues for each day in our analysis and the public agenda. In other words, in the case of ABC newscasts, Spearman rhos examined the agenda-setting effect on the public for time lags ranging from 1 day before our survey period to 180 days before our survey period. If agenda-setting effects are most pronounced after 1 day of coverage, for example, the Spearman rho for 1 day of coverage, the public agenda will be the largest in the study. The Spearman rhos also suggest where the public's memory decay occurs. If the Spearman rhos are no longer statistically significant after 30 days, for example, the results suggest that the public's memory of issue information decays after 30 days.

Several methodological aspects are important here. First, the methodology here employs an entire agenda of issues. This was the presupposition underscoring the original agenda-setting hypothesis—that an agenda of issues in the news media influences an agenda of issues that the public perceives as important. Thus, this analysis returns to the area proposed in the original agenda-setting hypothesis. Second, the analysis allows for the examination of several news media. Logically, information from different media is processed differently among individuals. The passive processing of visual information from television should produce results that are different from the active processing of verbal information from newspapers. Local information should also be processed differently than national information. Third, the analysis allows for the examination of several memory decay time lags. In other words, the analysis allows us to pinpoint to the day when the agenda-setting effect eventually decays in our study—from 1 day to 180 days.

The major shortcoming of this study is that the analysis, by design, uses aggregate data—that is, data from an entire public rather than from individuals. Thus, the memory decay examined here is not an individual's decay, but rather a decay from an entire population of individuals. Indeed, mental processes take place within individuals, not within a mass of individuals. However, agenda setting is a societal effect (see Lowery & DeFleur, 1988). Thus, memory decay, although taking place within individuals, should be apparent in an analysis of a population of individuals in which this process is occurring.

Differences Across Media.   According to the results, the ABC news broadcasts did not produce any statistically significant Spearman rhos for the 12 issues in this analysis. In other words, ABC news apparently did not have an agenda-setting effect on the respondents in this study.

This result is especially surprising because, logically, the national media should strongly match the public agenda because the agenda-setting

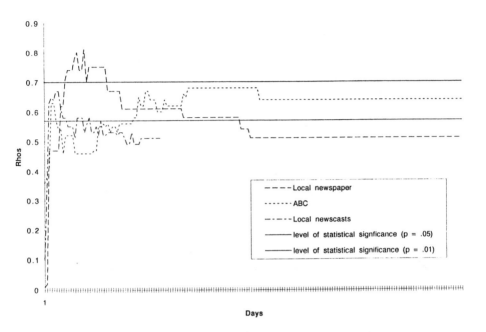

FIG. 6.1. Sperman rhos for three media.

question asks what the respondent believes is the most important problem facing our country today. The local media's concentration on local issues, on the other hand, should lessen their agenda-setting effect. A secondary analysis of the data revealed that one issue—international problems—received an extensive amount of coverage, but ranked low on the public agenda (a tie for tenth). Indeed, the nature of national network news implies that the networks provide extensive coverage of news around the world, which apparently did not catch the attention of respondents in the Eugene–Springfield survey.

Despite this quandary caused by the issue of international problems, several trends are apparent. The Spearman rank-order correlations for the national news broadcasts of ABC reached one of their highest levels at Day 4 and Day 5 ($r = .32$), before decreasing. Besides the first few days of the study, the lowest rho occurred after 14 days. The rhos showed a large increase again at Day 38 ($r = .36$) and reached their peak at Day 62 ($r = .39$). They remained at the .39 level until Day 92, when they dropped to .36 and remained at this point until the end of the study (Day 180).

To further examine the network television news–public relationship and to guard against the results of our study being suppressed because of coverage patterns for this one issue, we reanalyzed the data after dropping international problems from the analysis. The results of the 11 remaining issues mirrored the results of the original 12, except for the fact that statistically significant findings resulted at several points. The Spearman rank-order correlations are plotted in Fig. 6.1.

The Spearman rhos reached statistical significance after only four days ($r = .63$), and dropped below the $p < .05$ level of statistical significance after Day 6. The lowest rho was again at Day 14 ($r = .41$). The rhos reached statistical significance again at Day 38 ($r = .65$) and reached their peak at Day 62 ($r = .68$), before decreasing slightly at Day 92.

The Spearman rhos for local television broadcasts showed several differences from the rhos for national news. Here, the Spearman rhos reached statistical significance at Day 3 ($r = .63$) and peaked at Day 6 and Day 7 ($r = .67$). The rhos then decreased slightly, dropping below the level of statistical significance ($p < .05$) at Day 11 and reaching its lowest point at Day 14. The rhos again reached statistical significance from Day 15 to Day 17 and again at Day 20. All of the other rhos were not statistically significant at the $p < .05$ level. In addition, the rhos were unchanged from Day 42 through the end of the content analysis period at Day 50 ($r = .51$).

The Spearman rhos again were different for the local newspaper. The rhos reached statistical significance at Day 8 ($r = .62$). The rhos reached significance at the $p < .01$ level at Day 10 ($r = .71$), and peaked at both Day 15 and Day 18 ($r = .81$). The rhos dropped back to the $p < .05$ level at Day 28 ($r = .67$), before leveling off at Day 34 through Day 59 ($r = .61$). The rhos were no longer statistically significant at Day 84 ($r = .54$). The rhos were unchanged from Day 88 through the end of our study ($r = .51$).

Differential Mental Processing

Table 6.1 shows the overall results of the analysis here. The results demonstrate several differences in the mental processing of issue information in the print and broadcast media. A few similarities between the three media also emerged. First, agenda-setting effects were evident early for all three media. Effects appeared after 4 days for national network news (although only after the issue of international problems was dropped from the analysis), after 6 days for local news, and after 8 days for the local newspaper.

TABLE 6.1
Largest Rhos, Optimal Time Lags, and Memory Decay Time Periods for Three News Media

Medium	Largest Rho	Optimal Time Lags	Memory Decay Time Periods
National network news	.36/.32	62–91days/ 4–5 days	beyond 180 days/14 days
Local news broadcast	.67	6–7 days	14 days & 21 days
Local newspaper	.81	15 days & 18 days	28 days & 84 days

Second, the Spearman rank-order correlations showing agenda-setting effects dropped below statistically significant levels relatively quickly for all three news media. The rhos were no longer statistically significant after 6 days for ABC news and after 11 days for local newscasts. They reached their lowest level for both media at 14 days. Although the rhos for the local newspaper were statistically significant for a much longer time—until Day 85—the rhos dropped below the $p < .01$ level at Day 28. Thus, memory of issue information for local newspapers decayed slightly after 4 weeks, or in less than 2 weeks for the local and national broadcasts.

All of these results seem logical on the surface. Because individuals' long-term memory is limited, a memory decay of a few weeks after an initial agenda-setting effect of 4 to 8 days appears plausible. However, the agenda-setting effects, as demonstrated by the Spearman rank-order correlations, showed several differences for the three news media. Especially evident were differences in the magnitude of agenda-setting effects and differences in the long-term memory decay between the three news media examined here.

Newspapers had the most powerful agenda-setting influence, producing a rho of .81 ($p < .01$). Local broadcasts had the second strongest effect, with a peak rho of .67 ($p < .05$). National network broadcasts did not even produce a significant agenda-setting effect until the international problems issue was dropped from the analysis. With the international problems issue, the largest rho for the national network was just .36 ($p > .05$); without this issue, the network rho reached .68 ($p < .05$). Overall, then, newspapers had a more powerful agenda-setting effect than television, as both Tipton, Haney, and Basehart (1975) and McClure and Patterson (1976) found.

The agenda-setting effect for the local newspaper first appeared on Day 8 and peaked at Day 15 and Day 18. The agenda-setting effect decayed slightly at Day 28, and did not completely disappear until Day 85. Thus, the optimal time lag for agenda-setting effects to occur was longer for the local newspaper than for either local or national newscasts. The agenda-setting effect also decayed much more gradually for the local newspaper because the agenda-setting effect for both local and national broadcasts decayed only a short time after an early initial effect. This finding supports the argument of Shaw and McCombs (1977) that television news has a stronger short-term impact, but that newspapers have an effect across longer periods of time.

The agenda-setting effect decayed at much different rates for both local and national newscasts. The agenda-setting effect for local news broadcasts disappeared in Day 11, though there was a minor effect for Days 15 to 17 and Day 20. The agenda-setting effect disappeared completely by Day 21. For national news, it was not evident at all, until the issue of international problems was removed from the study. Then, the agenda-setting effect was evident for Days 4 and 5, but decayed by

Day 6. However, it reemerged at Day 38, then remained through the end of our study period, 180 days in all.

Two important points should be made about the results for the national newscasts. First, although an agenda-setting effect occurred early (Day 4 and 5), a consistent agenda-setting effect did not appear until Day 38, or more than 5 weeks before the survey period. Thus, the accumulated coverage of 5 weeks led to the most consistent agenda-setting effect for the ABC newscast. In addition, the optimal time lag for the strongest agenda-setting effects—when memory decay was accounted for—was between 62 and 92 days, or about 2 to 3 months before the survey period. Second, individuals' memory decay for national news broadcasts was very gradual. In fact, the findings suggest that the public's long-term memory decay of issue information went beyond the 6 months of news coverage examined in the present study.

One other possible explanation about the memory decay time period for the national network news should be noted: Perhaps agenda-setting effects really peaked at between 4 and 5 days, and memory of the issues decayed at Day 6. The consistent agenda-setting effect found after Day 38, then, may be due to the fact that coverage patterns finally stabilized here. Indeed, the media agenda changed little from Day 38 to Day 62 and did not change at all from Day 62 through Day 92 and from Day 92 through Day 180. It seems eminently logical that individuals' abilities to recall news coverage of issues should not last for 2 to 3 months. One week seems like a more logical time period for agenda-setting effects to occur, and 2 weeks seems like a logical time period for the memory of issue information to decay.

The results of local television news coverage, meanwhile, appeared to be more easily decipherable. Here, the optimal time lag for the strongest agenda-setting effects to occur was 6 to 7 days—or about 1 week. The memory decay of issue information followed 1 week later, with the Spearman rank-order correlations reaching one of their lowest points on Day 14 (when $r = .46$). Whereas agenda-setting effects again reached statistical significance on Day 15, none of the Spearman rhos after Day 21 were statistically significant.

Thus, taken as a whole, both local and national television news media and the local newspaper produced agenda-setting effects in a relatively short time. The memory of the issue information gained by respondents here also decayed in a relatively short time—much shorter than the Watt et al. (1993) study found. Overall, it should be noted that the findings should be tempered. Historical factors obviously cause time lag and memory decay differences at any given time. The optimal time lags and memory decay time periods found here, then, could be unique to the present study. Nonetheless, the results demonstrate that memory decay varies across different media, and these differences should be noted when determining time frames for agenda-setting studies. Greater precision in measuring time lags and memory decay time periods is imperative for future agenda-setting research.

7

The Role of Nonmedia Sources in the Agenda-Setting Process

Individuals can be concerned with a wide range of issues, from the price of groceries to conflicts in the Middle East. Individuals can also learn the relative importance of issues from a wide range of sources, from interpersonal communication to exposure to mass media.

Since the seminal study by McCombs and Shaw (1972), hundreds of studies have examined the influence of news media coverage on the public's issue priorities. The vast majority of these studies have indeed found strong correlations between the amount of coverage that issues received in the media and the public's level of concern with these same issues. Beyond the mass media, however, other sources of the public agenda, such as elected public officials, have received far less attention from communication researchers. How individuals learn the relative importance of the issues from different sources is an important question for public opinion scholars.

This chapter examines a potential nonmedia source of the public agenda, namely the president of the United States. This chapter compares the president–public agenda link with the media–public link, by examining public issue concerns after President Clinton's 1994 State of the Union address. In addition, two potential influences on the public agenda are examined: exposure to issue information and opinions about the source of the information, as measured by presidential approval ratings scores.

PUBLIC OFFICIALS AND THE NATIONAL AGENDA

Some evidence suggests that government officials can set the media's agenda in some situations (e. g., Atwater & Fico, 1986). Yet, relatively few studies have considered whether government leaders can directly affect the public's agenda via mediated communication, such as televised presidential speeches. One such study by Iyengar and Kinder (1987) found that on certain issues, the president influences the public's level of concern. Iyengar and Kinder, for example, found that when the president delivered national speeches dealing with energy, public concern with the issue of energy rose by more than 4%. On other issues, however, the president was less successful in influencing public concern and had to rely on the news media to put forth his issue priorities before the public.

Though agenda-setting researchers have devoted relatively little attention to the president–public relationship, several researchers have examined the president–media relationships. Wanta, Stephenson, Turk, and McCombs (1989) found that the president seemed to set media agendas in some situations and posited that presidential personality might serve as an intervening factor. Martin (1994) found, in his examination of budget proposal coverage by magazines, that presidential frames were not followed when they meshed with other media values. Hart (1987) argued that media translate presidential speeches as pegs for miniature dramas about issues. This chapter examines the president–press–public relationship by investigating the influence of the president and press on the public.

DATA ANALYSIS

The magnitude of influences from the mass media and the U.S. president were examined here. To examine the influences of the mass media, the agenda-setting susceptibility measure previously detailed was slightly modified. First, only data from the Eugene and Tampa surveys were included. The surveys at these two sites began in early February 1994, shortly after President Clinton's State of the Union address. The Jackson County study was conducted in November 1991, more than 2 months before the nearest State of the Union address.

Second, the issues included in the agenda-setting susceptibility measure were revised. The agenda-setting susceptibility measure utilized in previous chapters included the four issues that received the most coverage in the 4 weeks before the survey periods in our three sites. One of these issues was also one of the top three issues mentioned most prominently by President Clinton in his speech. Because the purpose of this chapter is to examine the relationships between the public and the president and press, only the three issues receiving heavy coverage and not mentioned prominently by the president were included in a news media coverage index.

To examine the influence of the president, three additional issue salience measures were computed. As previously mentioned, 12 issues were included in the issue concern section of our survey. The issues in this section included three issues that received extensive media coverage and were heavily emphasized in President Clinton's State of the Union address (crime, the economy, and health care), three issues that received extensive media coverage but were not emphasized in the State of the Union address (the environment, drug abuse, and race relations), three issues that received little coverage but received heavy emphasis in the State of the Union address (family values, welfare reform, and international problems) and three issues that received little media coverage and were not emphasized in the State of the Union address (the AIDS epidemic, homelessness, and unresponsive government).

The text of the State of the Union addresses was content analyzed to determine the degree of emphasis issues received in the speech. Lines in the text devoted to each issue and the number of stories devoted to the issues by the news media determined which of the four categories of issues each issue was placed in. Four issue concern measures were included in this analysis: a media issue concern measure, a presidential emphasis concern measure, a combined media–presidential concern measure and a nonmedia–nonpresidential issue concern measure.

Again, respondents were asked how concerned they were with each of the 12 issues—*extremely concerned, very concerned, somewhat concerned, a little concerned,* or *not concerned at all*. Scores for the three issues in each of the four sets of issues were summed. These scores, then, were an estimate of the respondents' concerns with each category of issues. The Cronbach's alphas ranged from .71 to .58.

Independent Variables. The exposure measure used for the mass media was identical to those detailed in earlier chapters.

The presidential exposure measure asked respondents if they happened to watch all, some, or none of President Clinton's State of the Union address.

Exposure to the State of the Union address was first correlated with the presidential issue concerns measure. Then, this variable was used as an independent variable in a regression analysis with the respondents' concern for the issues mentioned most prominently by the president in his State of the Union address as the dependent variable.

Statistical Tests. As with previous analyses, the variables were examined first through Pearson correlations, then through regression analyses.

Three additional analyses were computed. The first examined exposure to the news media and its influences on the respondents' concern with the set of issues that were covered heavily in the news media but not mentioned in the State of the Union address. This correlation was then compared to the correlation for the president exposure–presidential issue concern variables.

Next, the two exposure measures—to President Clinton's State of the Union address and to the mass media—were examined as independent variables in a regression analysis with the concern index for the issues receiving high media coverage and extensive emphasis in the State of the Union address. In other words, this final analysis compares which source has a stronger influence on the issue concern measure—the president or the news media.

Finally, the two exposure measures were examined as independent variables in a regression analysis with the concern index for issues that received little media coverage and little attention from President Clinton in his State of the Union address.

The President as Agenda Setter

The results of the Pearson correlations are listed in Table 7.1. Media exposure and exposure to the State of the Union address positively correlated with all four issue salience measures. Moreover, for all four issue salience measures, media exposure produced a stronger correlation than did exposure to the State of the Union address—including the correlation involving the issues emphasized by President Clinton in his speech but not covered in the news media.

Table 7.2 details the results of the regression analysis examining media influence on issues receiving extensive media coverage. As the table shows, media exposure (p = .000) was a significant predictor of issue salience. Results of the examination of the influences of President Clinton on the issues receiving extensive emphasis in his State of the Union address are detailed in Table 7.3. Here, exposure to the State of the Union address (p = .005) was a significant predictor of issue salience.

TABLE 7.1

Pearson Correlations Examining the Relationships Between Exposure Variables and Issue Concern Measures

Variable	Media Exposure	President Exposure
Media only issues	.150***	.100*
President only issues	.242***	.120**
Media–president issues	.190***	.111**
Neither media–president issues	.134**	.092*

Note. *p < .05; **p < .01; ***p < .001.

TABLE 7.2

Regression Analysis Results for the Influence of Media Exposure on Concern for Issues Covered Heavily in the News Media

Variable	Beta	Significance
Media exposure	.150	.001

Note. Multiple R = .150; R-Square = .022; Adjusted R-Square = .021.

Table 7.4 lists the results of the regression analysis examining simultaneous influence of the press and president on respondents' concerns for issues that both received extensive coverage in the media and heavy emphasis in President Clinton's State of the Union address. The results demonstrate the dominance of media influence. When both independent variables were examined simultaneously, only the media exposure variable ($p = .000$) was a significant predictor of issue salience.

Finally, Table 7.5 shows the results of the regression analyses examining influences on the public for issues that received both little media coverage and little emphasis in President Clinton's State of the Union address. Only exposure to media was a significant predictor of issue salience. However, it should be noted that the explained variance is the smallest of the four tests.

Exposure and Effects. Many of the findings here were expected. First, exposure to messages dealing with issues led to higher issue salience. In other words, respondents who exposed themselves to messages trans-

TABLE 7.3
Regression Analysis Results for the Influence of Exposure to President Clinton's State of the Union Address on Concern for Issues Mentioned Prominently in His Speech

Variable	Beta	Significance
Presidential exposure	.119	.005

Note. Multiple $R = .119$; R-Square $= .014$; Adjusted R-Square $= .013$.

TABLE 7.4
Regression Analysis Results for the Influence of Media Exposure and Presidential Exposure on Concern for Issues Covered Heavily in the News Media and Mentioned Prominently in the State of the Union Address

Variable	Beta	Significance
Media exposure	.173	.000
Presidential exposure	.065	.136

Note. Multiple $R = .199$; R-Square $= .040$; Adjusted R-Square $= .036$.

TABLE 7.5
Regression Analysis Results for the Influence of Media Exposure and Presidential Exposure on Concern for Issues Receiving Little Coverage in the News Media and Little Mention in the State of the Union Address

Variable	Beta	Significance
Media exposure	.121	.006
Presidential exposure	.054	.228

Note. Multiple $R = .144$; R-Square $= .021$; Adjusted R-Square $= .017$.

mitted by both the media and the president were likely to believe that the issues mentioned in their messages were important. Thus, these findings support the notion of a simple message transferral model of agenda setting. Through coverage of certain issues by the media and through emphasis of certain issues by the president in his State of the Union address, respondents were exposed to issue salience cues. The more exposure respondents had to the salience cues, the more respondents felt these issues were important problems facing our country.

In addition, exposure to the media and President Clinton's State of the Union address had less of an effect in influencing the perceived importance of issues that received little coverage and little mention in the president's speech. In other words, respondents who believed that these ignored issues were important must have received salience cues from sources other than the media and the president. Thus, exposure to the media and the president's speech, logically, should have relatively little influence on the perceived importance for these issues—as was the case in this analysis. As the results show, the two exposure variables, whereas statistically significant predictors of issue concern, explained relatively little of the variance of this dependent variable.

The final result produced was somewhat less expected, namely that when the levels of exposure to the president's speech and the press were compared simultaneously, press exposure was the dominant predictor variable. In other words, for issues that received both extensive coverage in the news media and high emphasis in the president's speech, the exposure level to the news media was a stronger predictor of issue salience than was the exposure level to the State of the Union address.

Two explanations for this finding seem plausible. First, the finding could be due to the methodology employed here. Exposure to the news media was measured through an index of three items. Exposure to President Clinton's State of the Union address was measured through a single item with only three response categories. Thus, the media exposure measure displayed a great deal more variance than the measure of exposure to the president's State of the Union address. Second, the finding could be due to the three-way relationship between the president, press, and public. The president may need the news media to further highlight and explain the issues that he deemed important. Without the news media to transmit further information dealing with issues, the president, through his State of the Union address, only has one chance to influence the perceived importance of issues held by the public. Thus, the president needs the daily repetition of news media coverage to advance the agenda of issues that he deemed important.

Beyond the question of mere exposure to messages, psychological variables may also play a role in the development of issue salience. Opinions about the source of issue information, as previous chapters detailed, perform an important function in the development of issue salience. Thus, factors influencing the perceived effectiveness of the president is an important consideration in the agenda-setting process.

The Effects of Attitudes Toward the President

Although the news media appears to have a stronger influence on the public than the president, a secondary analysis was conducted to examine whether the president has a different influence on the public than an agenda-setting effect. Thus, an attitudinal variable—the respondents' approval or disapproval of the president—was included in a secondary analysis of presidential influence. This final analysis examined whether the president had an agenda-setting effect or a priming influence.

On the surface, the concepts of agenda setting and priming appear to be very similar. Both concepts predict strong effects of the mass media on the public. Both concepts propose that story selection affects audience evaluations by influencing the likelihood that certain issues come to mind when evaluating either issue importance or the approval of public officials.

However, the final outcomes of the two concepts—the eventual effects of the exposure to the messages—are drastically different. Agenda setting is based on the notion that the press does not necessarily tell people what to think, but rather what to think about. Thus, exposure to mass media coverage of issues influences the perceived importance of these issues held by media consumers. Therefore, the mass media influence issue salience.

Priming, however, proposes a much stronger effect of the mass media. Priming is based on the notion that the press does tell people what to think. By including certain stories and excluding others, the media show certain individuals, such as public officials, in different lights. Thus, good news about the economy, for example, increases the likelihood that members of the public view President Clinton in a positive way.

Mass communication researchers, of course, have found support for both agenda setting and priming. The purpose here, however, is to test the two concepts simultaneously. The present analysis examines these two concepts—agenda setting and priming—using a series of path analyses.

THEORETICAL FRAMEWORK

Priming

Priming assumes that there are many competing sets of cognitive systems in one's mind that cannot be processed at the same time. External cues "prime" a particular set or sets of such systems to be used to make judgments or decisions (Anderson & Bower, 1973; McNamara,

1992). Schleuder, McCombs, and Wanta (1992) provided a good example involving an ambiguous word such as *bank*. Shortly after a person watches a news story on savings and loans, the word is likely to be associated with a financial institution rather than a side of a river.

Facing a judgment or choice, people are not likely to take all plausible considerations into account, carefully examine and weigh all their implications, and finally integrate them all into a summary decision. Instead, they tend to be cognitive misers and rely on information that is most accessible in memory (Kaheman, Slovic, & Tversky, 1982; Krosnick & Kinder, 1990). Such external cues often come from the mass media.

With both experiments and surveys (Iyengar & Kinder, 1987; Iyengar, Peters, Kinder, & Krosnick, 1984; Krosnick & Kinder, 1990), researchers found that the media's coverage of certain issues influence how people judge the overall performance of public officials. For example, media reports of the Iran-Contra controversy primed the public to evaluate President Reagan's overall performance based on this particular issue (Krosnick & Kinder, 1990). Thus, politicians have been trying to influence the media's agenda in order to prime the public with issues that are most beneficial to themselves (Jacobs & Shapiro, 1994; Mendelsohn, 1994).

Agenda Setting Versus Priming

Superficially, priming appears to be an additional stage in the agenda-setting process. Here, the media's agenda primes the audience to make judgments about public officials. In other words, agenda setting occurs before priming. Thus, exposure to the media leads to issue salience, which, in turn, affects individuals' attitudes toward the president.

Studies on the president's agenda-setting influence, however, suggests a different model. Research shows that the more popular a president is, the more likely he is to influence the public (Wanta, 1991). In other words, attitudes toward the president influence how effective he is in getting the public to be concerned with his issue priorities.

Agenda setting proposes that exposure to messages on issues leads to a certain attitude toward issues (issue salience). The variable of president popularity (the audience's attitude toward the information source) intervenes between exposure and agenda-setting effects. In other words, exposure to the State of the Union address might influence an audience's attitude to the source of messages—namely, the president. Such an attitude can determine a message's impact on the audience, with the audience's issue salience as the end result. Simply put, how much people approve of the job that the president is doing may influence how important they think certain issues are—when the issues are emphasized by the president.

Priming, however, argues for a different process. Priming does not place attitudes toward the president in the middle of the process. Rather, such evaluations are the end result of a cognitive process. In other words, people are exposed to issue information first. Then, they decide which issues are important and ultimately use those issues as references to evaluate the president.

Several researchers have linked agenda setting and priming. As Price and Tewksbury (1995) noted, priming is based on the tendency of individuals to use the issues receiving extensive coverage as criteria for judging the performance of political leaders. Agenda setting is based on the tendency of individuals to use news media coverage as salience cues for judging the importance of individual issues. Thus, priming and agenda setting are based on the notion that story selection affects media consumers through knowledge activation. As Price and Tewksbury (1995) wrote:

> Essential to both processes is the idea that story selection affects audience evaluations via an intermediate impact on knowledge activation, that is by influencing the likelihood that some issues rather than others will come to mind, thus affecting audience judgment about issue importance or approval of public actors.

Thus, the main question addressed here is which gets activated first: issue information or attitudinal information? If issue information is activated first, it ultimately influences the attitudes of individuals regarding the president—as the concept of priming suggests. If attitudinal information is activated first, it ultimately influences the salience of issues emphasized by the source of the information—as the concept of agenda setting suggests.

Thus, because agenda setting and priming predict different final outcomes, two models of influence can be proposed utilizing these two concepts. These models are depicted in Fig. 7.1.

An Agenda-Setting Model. In the first step of the agenda-setting model of presidential influence, individuals form opinions about the president based on prior experience and information. Based on their opinions of the president, they then expose themselves to messages from the president. In other words, if individuals think highly of the job President Clinton is doing, they are very likely to watch all or most of the State of the Union address. Finally, based on the amount of exposure individuals have to President Clinton's speech, they develop concerns with the issues that he stressed in the State of the Union address. High exposure to the speech leads to high concern with the issues mentioned in the speech. The end product of this model of presidential influence is issue salience.

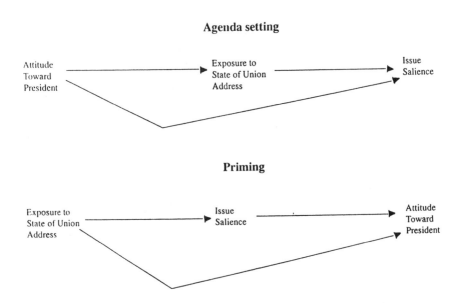

FIG. 7.1. Models of presidential influence.

A Priming Model.   The priming model of influence is markedly different. The first stage of the priming model deals with exposure levels.
Next, individuals form opinions about the issues stressed by the source
of the information based on their exposure to the source. Finally, based
on their opinions about the issues emphasized by a source, individuals
form attitudes toward the source of the information.

Thus, a priming model of presidential influence begins with exposure
to the State of the Union address. High exposure to President Clinton's
State of the Union address leads individuals to believe the issues
stressed in his speech are important. Finally, the individuals' level of
issue salience affects how they ultimately feel about the president. In
other words, individuals who believe the issues emphasized by the
president in his State of the Union address are important, then believe
the president is doing a good job.

One final point should be noted about the priming model. Although
exposure to media issue coverage is a prerequisite for priming to take
place, the priming concept is modified to include direct exposure to
presidential issues and messages. Thus, the model involves exposure to
the president's State of the Union address—and not exposure to news
media coverage. Logically, the priming model should show stronger
presidential influence on the public because individuals are directly
exposed to presidential issue priorities.

As Fig. 7.1 details, this analysis basically tests which situation occurs
last: attitude toward the president/media or issue salience. Agenda

setting suggests that issue salience is the final outcome of these communication effects models. Priming, however, suggests that attitudes
toward the source of the information is the final outcome of the model.

Priming and the President

Figure 7.2 displays the results of the path analysis tests of the
agenda-setting and priming models. As Fig. 7.2 shows, the data fit the
priming model better than the agenda-setting model for presidential
influence. Both presidential models produced two statistically significant path coefficients.

In the agenda-setting model, the paths from attitude toward president and exposure to the State of the Union address to issue salience
were statistically significant. In the priming model, the path from
exposure to the State of the Union address to issue salience and the path
from issue salience to attitude toward the president were statistically
significant. However, the path coefficients were generally larger in the
priming model than in the agenda-setting model. In addition, the
significant paths form a logical linear progression in the priming model:
from exposure to the State of the Union address to concern with the
issues in the address to attitudes toward the president.

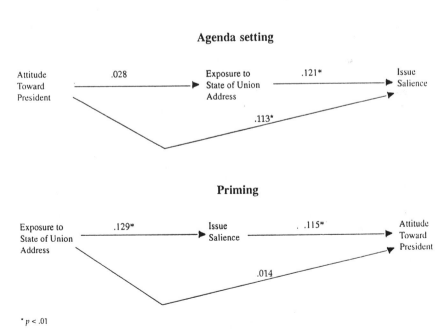

FIG. 7.2. Presidential influence results.

Thus, the results clearly offer stronger support for the priming model of presidential influence. Here, exposure to the State of the Union address influenced how concerned individuals were with the issues emphasized in President Clinton's 1994 State of the Union speech. High exposure to the State of the Union speech led to high concern with the issues mentioned in the speech. Exposure activated knowledge of issue importance first in the presidential influence model.

Next, concern with the issues mentioned in the State of the Union address influenced individuals' attitudes toward the president. If individuals were highly concerned with the same issues that President Clinton stressed in his speech, they were likely to think President Clinton was doing a good job as president. Thus, the final outcome of this model was a more positive attitude toward the president, as the priming model argues. Knowledge of attitudes about the president was activated last in this model.

The agenda-setting model of presidential influence, although producing two statistically significant path coefficients, nonetheless, was somewhat less supported through the tests here. Individuals' levels of exposure to the State of the Union address were not related to their attitudes toward President Clinton. Individuals' levels of exposure to President Clinton's speech and their attitudes toward the president both led to concern with the issues stressed in his speech. However, these two variables affected issue salience simultaneously and did not demonstrate a clear linear progression as did the presidential priming model. In addition, the path coefficients in the priming model (.129 and .115) were larger than the coefficients in the agenda-setting model (.121 and .113). Again, the findings suggest that the data fit the priming model better than the agenda-setting model on the tests of presidential influence on the public.

It should be noted that the analysis of the president might have improved by utilizing measures that allowed for more variance. Both exposure to the State of the Union address and attitudes toward the president were based on a 3-point scale. The results might have been stronger had more rigorous measures been used that produced a wider range of response categories.

In addition, the agenda-setting model of presidential influence was based largely on previous work in media influence (Wanta, Hu, & Miller, 1994). Perhaps, however, the agenda-setting model was inappropriate for a study of presidential influence (e.g., perhaps attitudes about the president did not precede exposure to presidential messages). Possibly, individuals did not come to the State of the Union address with set, preconceived notions about the president, as they did when deciding their exposure levels for the mass media. In other words, perhaps individuals watched the State of the Union address with an open mind about the president and formed opinions based on his performance in the speech. Thus, exposure precedes attitudes. Indeed, this could be the case of a significant segment of the respondents here.

On the other hand, individuals may look at the news media in a different way. They may not use the news media with an open mind and may not form their attitudes on the media based on this exposure. In the case of the news media, attitudes precede exposure. Thus, the nature of the public's relationships may greatly differ between the media and the president.

In addition, the priming model, unlike previous priming studies, only included exposure to the president. Media exposure and media coverage were not examined. The magnitude of the priming model results found here may be partially due to the exposure measure. Exposure to the president's State of the Union address ultimately led respondents to view the president in a positive light. This suggests that the president does not necessarily need the news media to prime the public into viewing him in a positive way. The president can prime the public directly, through major televised speeches, such as the State of the Union address.

The models, nonetheless, demonstrate clear trends for the variables examined. According to the results, priming explains the relationship between the president and the public better than agenda setting. The end product of this relationship—again, the final stage of knowledge activation—is an individual's attitude toward the president, or a higher opinion of the president.

Overall, the findings here demonstrate that the public, news media, and president are intertwined in a complex three-way relationship. Much more work needs to be done to fully understand how these three actors interact.

8

Expanding the
Agenda-Setting Hypothesis

The majority of agenda-setting research through the years has concentrated on how media coverage of issues influences the perceived importance of those same issues among members of the public. Thus, the dependent variable in these studies has been issue salience, or how issues rank in perceived importance on the public's agenda.

This chapter involves a new application of agenda setting by examining an effect different from that proposed in the traditional agenda-setting hypothesis. Rather than look at one specific issue that individuals are concerned with, this analysis looks at the number of issues that individuals are concerned with—in other words, the agenda diversity of individuals.

This analysis argues that the news media has an additional effect on people from the one that the original agenda-setting hypothesis predicts. If exposure to the news media influences the perceived importance of issues by individuals, high levels of exposure gives individuals cues that a diverse agenda of issues is important. Thus, not only do individuals learn the relative importance of issues through the coverage they receive in the news media, but they also become concerned with more issues if they have high levels of exposure to media messages. Therefore, exposure to the news media increases issue diversity within individuals.

As with the concept of agenda setting, several factors influence the number of issues concerning individuals. Why individuals read a newspaper could also influence the number of issues with which they are concerned. The uses and gratifications measures (Becker, 1979), therefore, could be an important determinant of issue diversity. Individuals who read newspapers "to keep up with the latest events " or "to determine what is important" are more likely to be concerned with many issues than individuals who feel a low need in these areas. In addition, demographics could influence the level of issue diversity held by individuals. Because older, higher educated individuals with higher incomes tend to read newspapers more often than younger, lower educated individuals with low incomes (Stone, 1987), they should also tend to be concerned with more issues because of their high media exposure.

Two purposes guide this analysis. First, the influence of three sets of variables on the number of issue concerns held by individuals are examined. The variables—which include demographics, media use motivations, and exposure to news media—are examined through a series of regression analyses. Second, a model is proposed and tested based on the results of the regression analyses. The model, which employs a hierarchical regression analysis, examines the relative strengths of the demographic, motivational, and media usage variables on the number of issue concerns held by individuals.

THEORETICAL FRAMEWORK

Since the seminal study by McCombs and Shaw (1972), the vast majority of agenda-setting research has supported the notion that members of the public learn the relative importance of issues through coverage the issues receive in the news media. Researchers have found considerably less support for the agenda-setting hypothesis when utilizing what McCombs (1981) called a *Type II approach*—that is, investigations with the individual (rather than the issue) as the unit of measurement, including an entire set of issues (rather than one issue). McCombs, however, noted that only a very few studies conducted this type of analysis.

Similarly, few studies have attempted to examine *issue diversity*, or whether respondents could be concerned with a wide range of issues. McCombs and Zhu (1994) examined long-term trends in issue agendas of public through three variables: increases in agenda capacity, increases in agenda diversity, and increases in issue volatility. Although they found no significant linear increase in capacity, the results provide strong evidence of increases in both diversity and volatility from 1939 through 1994. They concluded that the volatility of contemporary public opinion was the result of two forces: the expansive influence of education on awareness of public issues and the constraint imposed by the public agenda's limited capacity.

Ferguson (1984) and Allen and Izcaray (1988) also examined if the public agenda increased its capacity over time. Both studies found that the total number of issues named per person expanded over time. This formulation corresponded to what Allen and Izcaray termed *nominal agenda diversity*.

One factor affecting the number of issues people are concerned with could be the number of media available to the news consumers. Chaffee and Wilson (1977), for example, examined individuals who resided in media-rich areas, those in which several news media were readily available, and media-poor areas. They found support for their hypothesis that having more news media available leads individuals to voice concern with a more diverse agenda of issues.

Thus, if, as Chaffee and Wilson (1977) found, the more media that are available, the wider the range of issues with which members in a community will be concerned, perhaps a related hypothesis could also be true: The more media content that is consumed, the more issues with which individuals will be concerned. If issue information varies to some degree in various news media, individuals will receive more salience cues as their consumption of media content increases. In other words, if individuals often read several newspapers, watch network news, and watch local news, they will be exposed to a wide range of issues calling for their attention. The more media information individuals consume, the more issues they are exposed to. High media exposure should translate into concern with several issues.

Beyond media consumption, however, are further questions of the type of individuals who voice concern with many issues. Individuals with a high interest in political news, for example, are likely to expose themselves to high levels of news content, and, in turn, are likely to believe many issues are important. In addition, because Hill (1985) found that agenda-setting effects were most likely to be found among those individuals most interested in and attentive to news, perhaps individuals with strong interests in political news are also most likely to have diverse issue concerns.

Other motivations for using the news media may also influence the number of issue concerns for individuals. As researchers examining individuals' uses and gratifications would argue, selection of media messages is based on which content provides the most utility or interests individuals the most. Thus, individuals may seek out news stories to help them determine what issues are important. Individuals with strong motivations to keep informed may also have high exposure to the news media and therefore high exposure to many issues, which, in turn, leads individuals to become concerned with many issues.

Finally, demographics influence issue concern frequency. Previous studies have found that education, age, and income are all correlated with increased newspaper usage (Stone, 1987). If older individuals with higher education and income levels use newspapers often, they are exposed to a wide range of issues calling for their attention. Thus, it is likely that these demographic variables are also correlated with the number of issues about which respondents voice concern. In addition, age and education especially seem likely to influence issue diversity. Older individuals have been exposed to more issues through the years, so they should be concerned with several issues. In other words, personal involvement with issues through the years may lead to stronger issue diversity within older individuals.

Popkin (1991), meanwhile, argued that education may lead to issue diversity "by increasing the number of issues that citizens see as politically relevant, and by increasing the number of connections they make between their own lives and national and international events" (p. 36). This broadening of the electorate through education has been especially significant in recent years, given the extensive expansion of education in the United States since World War II.

DATA ANALYSIS

Data came from a second telephone survey conducted in Jackson County, Illinois. This survey was conducted in November 1991. The selection of respondents and the interviewing methodology were identical to the 1990 survey used for the previous analyses. An entirely new survey was utilized in the 1991 study, however.

Dependent Variable. This variable includes the number of issue concerns. Respondents were asked the traditional agenda-setting question, "What do you think is the number one problem facing our country today?" Respondents were then asked, "Are there any other problems that you think are very important?" and "Any other problems?" until the respondents stopped mentioning issues. Thus, respondents could mention an infinite number of issues. Responses ranged from 0 to 6. This raw score then formed the dependent variable of issue diversity.

Independent Variables. Independent variables are media exposure, uses and gratifications motivations, and demographics. The media exposure variables asked respondents how many days in a typical week they read a newspaper, watched local television news, and watched national network news. Because the area surveyed had a number of newspapers readily available, and because readers of more than one newspaper would likely be exposed to a wider variety of issues, respondents were also asked how many newspapers they read at least twice a week.

The motivation measures were determined by responses to the traditional uses and gratification items proposed by Becker (1979). Respondents were asked if they strongly agreed, agreed, were undecided, disagreed, or strongly disagreed with the following reasons they read a newspaper: to keep up with the latest events, to determine what is important, to obtain useful information for daily life, to help me form opinions about things going on around me, to help me make decisions on issues, just to pass the time, to understand what's going on, to be entertained, to give me something to talk about with other people, to use in my discussions with friends, because I agree with editorial stands, to strengthen my arguments on issues, to feel I am participating in current events, and for information in advertisements.

A final motivation variable in the analysis involved an index developed by McCombs and Poindexter (1983). This "civic duty " index was formed by adding responses of the *strongly agree* to *strongly disagree* scale for the following: "We have a duty to keep ourselves informed about news and current events;" "It is important to be informed about news and current events;" "So many other people follow the news and keep informed about it that it does not matter much whether I do or not;" and "A good deal of news about current events is not important enough to keep informed about." The Cronbach's alpha for this index was .81.

The demographic questions asked respondents their education level, age, and income. The respondents' gender was recorded at the conclusion of the survey by interviewers.

Statistical Tests. Two sets of statistical tests were conducted. First, a series of stepwise regression analyses examined the relationships between the three sets of independent variables and the dependent variable (issue diversity). The stepwise regression separately examined each of the three sets of independent variables: demographics, motivations, and media use.

Second, a hierarchical regression examined issue diversity and all of the variables found statistically significant in the three previous regression analyses. Only significant variables from the three regression analyses were included in the final hierarchical regression. The hierarchical regression allowed for an examination of the relative strengths of all of the independent variables on issue diversity.

Factors Affecting Agenda Diversity

Table 8.1 lists the regression results for the demographic variables. Age was positively related to issue diversity. Thus, the older that the respondents were, the more issues they were concerned with. Education, income, and gender were not related to the number of issue concerns.

The results examining the motivation variables are detailed in Table 8.2. Only two variables were entered into the regression equation. According to the results, whether or not individuals read newspapers for information in advertising was negatively related to issue diversity and whether or not individuals felt a strong civic duty to read the newspaper was positively related to issue diversity. In other words, the more respondents read newspapers for information about advertisements, the fewer issues they were concerned with, and the stronger respondents felt a civic duty to keep informed, the more issues they were concerned with.

TABLE 8.1
Regression Analysis Results for Demographic Variables on Issue Diversity

Variables	Beta	Significance
Age	.13	.0107
Nonsignificant variables		
Education		
Income		
Gender		

Note. Multiple $R = .13$; R-square $= .02$.

TABLE 8.2
Regression Analysis Results for Motivational Variables on Issue Diversity

Variables	Beta	Significance
Use newspapers for information in ads	-.20	.0001
Civic duty index	.20	.0001
Nonsignificant variables		
To keep up with events		
To determine what is important		
To obtain useful information		
To help me form opinions		
To help me make decisions on issues		
To pass the time		
To understand what's going on		
To be entertained		
To give me something to talk about		
To use in my discussions with friends		
Because I agree with editorial stands		
To strengthen my arguments on issues		
To feel I am participating in current events		

Note. Multiple $R = .24$; R-square $= .06$.

Table 8.3 lists the results of the media exposure variables. As the table shows, only one of the four media exposure variables was entered into the regression equation. The results show that the number of newspapers that respondents read was a significant predictor of the number of issue concerns that they voiced.

All four variables that were significant predictors of issue diversity remained statistically significant when they were examined simultaneously, as Table 8.4 shows. Age was the strongest predictor, followed by the number of newspapers read, and the civic duty index. Whether or not respondents used newspapers for information in advertisements, the weakest predictor, was negatively related to issue diversity.

From the regression analyses, several conclusions are apparent. First, media usage, as expected, was an important variable in predicting individuals' level of issue diversity. Specifically, if individuals read more newspapers, they tended to voice more issue concerns, likely because they were exposed to a variety of issues in the different newspapers. The

TABLE 8.3
Regression Analysis Results for Media Exposure Variables on Issue Diversity

Variables	Beta	Significance
Number of newspapers read	.22	.000
Nonsignificant variables		
Days watching local news		
Days reading a newspaper		
Days watching national news		

Note. Multiple $R = .22$; R-square $= .05$.

TABLE 8.4
Regression Analysis Results for All Variables on Issue Diversity

Variables	Beta	Significance
Age	.13	.0114
Use newspapers for information in ads	-.11	.0363
Civic duty index	.13	.0202
Number of newspapers read	.13	.0138

Note. Multiple $R = .26$; R-square $= .07$.

more newspapers individuals were exposed to, the more issues they thought were important.

Frequency of reading newspapers and watching television news, on the other hand, were not significant predictors in the regression analyses. It should be noted, however, that both frequency of reading newspapers ($r = .23$; $p < .001$) and frequency of watching television news ($r = .13$; $p < .05$) correlated with issue diversity. Nonetheless, according to the tests conducted here, consumption of a variety of media was a stronger predictor of issue diversity than mere exposure to news media.

This supports the finding of Chaffee and Wilson (1977), who found that individuals in communities with the availability of several media (media-rich areas) voiced concern with a wider variety of issues than individuals in communities in media-poor areas. Apparently, the diversity of media consumed by individuals leads to issue diversity within news consumers. Obviously, this finding appears logical. If individuals consume diverse messages from the news media, they will be concerned with a diverse agenda of issues. Thus, the consumption of a wide variety of media leads to a larger number of issues with which people will be concerned.

Also as expected, age was a positive predictor of issue diversity. Because older individuals have been exposed to more issues through their lifetimes and because they use newspapers more often than younger individuals, older respondents voiced concern with more issues than younger respondents. Thus, exposure to issues through the years also increases the likelihood of individuals being concerned with a wide range of issues.

Two variables examining respondents' motivations to use the news media were significant predictors of issue diversity. Individuals who felt a strong motivation to read newspapers for information in advertisements voiced few issue concerns. Thus, individuals motivated to use the news media for reasons other than news had less diverse issue agendas. The content of the media that individuals consume plays an important role in determining individuals' exposure to issues and thus the diversity of issues with which they become concerned. Therefore, advertising consumption means individuals are attending to information other than that contained in issue-oriented news stories. Advertising consumers are not exposing themselves to salience cues contained in news stories and thus tend to think that fewer issues are important.

The civic duty index was positively related to issue concern frequency, as one would expect. If individuals felt a strong duty to keep informed on important issues, they also voiced their concern with many issues. Indeed, civic duty and issue concerns appeared to be closely linked. Individuals who feel a strong duty to keep informed about their community likely have many concerns about their community.

Overall, then, older individuals who find low utility in advertising information but who read a variety of newspapers and feel a strong civic duty to keep informed are likely to believe there are many important issues facing the United States today.

These findings point to the need for further research in this area. The dependent variable examined here—issue diversity—is an important consideration worthy of further attention from mass communication scholars. This analysis was an attempt to expand the agenda-setting hypothesis in a new direction. In two decades of research, scholars have considerably expanded the model of the agenda-setting process by examining a host of audience and message variables (e.g., Hill, 1985; Wanta & Wu, 1992; Zhu, 1992; Zucker, 1978) and a considerable number of antecedent variables explaining the formation of the news agenda.

However, the outcome of this process, the public agenda, essentially remained fixed in the form first articulated by McCombs and Shaw (1972), a description of public issues in terms of salience. That situation is now changing as researchers are now investigating numerous facets of the public agenda (Carter, Stamm, & Heintz-Knowles, 1992; Edelstein, 1993; Zhu, 1992).

Agenda-setting studies have been concerned with which issues were on the public agenda. This research expands the portrait of public opinion by examining how many issues are on the public agenda. This expanded portrait of the public agenda enhances our understanding of the marketplace of ideas and informs the continuing debate about which features of that marketplace create the diversity of views that ensure the well being of democracies.

9

Social Learning in the Agenda-Setting Process

In the seminal agenda-setting article, McCombs and Shaw (1972) pointed out that individual differences in the judgments of the voters may have been lost by grouping all of their respondents together in the data analysis. They also noted that the correlations between voter and media agendas were not uniform across all groups of voters, suggesting that differences existed between individuals in their study. They thus recommended that subsequent agenda-setting research move from a broad societal level to the social psychological level by comparing individuals' concerns with individuals' use of mass media. This book is an attempt to do just that. A quarter of a century has now passed since McCombs and Shaw published the first test of the agenda-setting hypothesis. An in-depth individual-level analysis of this important area of mass communication research has been long in coming.

As the previous chapters demonstrated, agenda setting is a complex process of social learning in which media consumers take part as active participants. As with formal academic education, several factors influence the social learning of issue salience that is at the heart of agenda setting.

From the preceding chapters, a more focused portrait of the individual most likely to display agenda-setting effects has emerged. In general, this type of person is highly educated, highly interested in politics and believes the news media are watching out for the public's welfare.

Furthermore, the agenda-setting effect goes through several stages. Individuals first form opinions about the mass media based on their demographic backgrounds. They then form a reliance on the mass media based on their attitudes toward the media. Individuals then adjust their behavioral patterns based on their level of reliance on the media. Finally, individuals become susceptible to agenda-setting influences based on their previous behavior.

Outside factors also come into play in this agenda-setting process. Individuals can get salience cues from nonmedia sources. The results here show that if individuals are exposed to major national speeches, they become concerned with issues emphasized by important public officials. The influence of these public officials, however, is not as powerful as the media's influence, suggesting that public officials need the news media to continue transmitting information about issues stressed in their speeches long after the speeches are delivered. This repetition of issue information is important and necessary.

In addition, public officials can have an additional effect on individuals beyond agenda setting. The data here show stronger support for a priming model of presidential influence than an agenda-setting model of presidential influence. Exposure to major, nationally televised speeches can influence how people view important public officials.

From this standpoint, then, several conclusions can be drawn about the agenda-setting process.

• Individuals most able to understand the significance of the mass media's coverage of issues are also most likely to be affected by this coverage.

Indeed, research in the knowledge gap hypothesis suggests this finding. As researchers of the knowledge gap hypothesis argue, acquisition of knowledge proceeds at a faster rate among better-educated individuals than among those with less education. Thus, highly educated individuals learn more from media messages than individuals with low education levels, creating an ever-widening gap in knowledge. They cite five reasons for this differential learning (see Tichenor, Donohue, & Olien, 1970).

1. Highly educated individuals are better equipped to efficiently process and comprehend information contained in media messages. That is, highly educated people have better communication processing skills.
2. Highly educated individuals have more stored information. Thus, they have extensive relevant information in their memory with which to use in processing new information.
3. Highly educated people tend to have more relevant social contacts. Therefore, they might associate with people who are also exposed to public affairs and might enter into discussions with them on these topics.
4. Individuals may selectively expose themselves to information from the news media. Individuals with low levels of education simply might not want to attend to information in the news media.
5. The mass media system itself is geared toward individuals of high socioeconomic status. Much media coverage is oriented toward the interests of highly educated individuals. Much media content is written at a level that is inaccessible to people with low educational backgrounds.

These findings suggest a pattern similar to results found in knowledge gap research. All five of these reasons for the existence of a knowledge gap explain why the agenda-setting effect was strongest among highly educated individuals in this study.

Highly educated individuals process and comprehend information about important issues more efficiently than individuals with low education levels. More education means a more refined mental processing system with which to evaluate media salience cues transmitted through news coverage.

Highly educated individuals also have more stored knowledge to utilize in assessing the significance of the issue coverage. Thus, education provides individuals with a better basis for evaluating the significance of issue salience cues in relation to previous media coverage. In addition, highly educated individuals may have more social contacts with which to discuss issue coverage. Interpersonal communication, as we have seen, can enhance agenda-setting effects.

Individuals with low education may not find information about public affairs compatible with their values and/or attitudes. Therefore, they may be selective in their exposure to media messages.

Finally, because media messages are geared for highly educated media consumers, individuals with low education levels may be uninterested in issue coverage. They may not attend to media messages because they do not think media messages are useful or pertinent to them. Thus, highly educated individuals would naturally learn the social significance of issue coverage from the news media better than individuals with low education would. These findings bear out that conclusion. Instead of a knowledge gap, however, these results suggest an issue salience gap. Individuals with high levels of education learn the relative importance of issues more efficiently than individuals with low levels of education.

• Individuals with high motivations to gain information about important issues are most likely to be influenced by the mass media's coverage of those issues.

As these results demonstrate, the psychological makeup of individuals plays an important role in the agenda-setting process. Three factors could be at work here. First, this result could be related to the concept of the need for orientation. As noted earlier, the need for orientation is based mainly on two factors: the perceived relevance of a message's content and the perceived uncertainty about the subject of the message. High relevance and high uncertainty lead to a high need for orientation. High relevance and low uncertainty lead to a moderate need for orientation. Thus, if an issue appears to be relevant to an individual, she or

he demonstrate either a high or moderate need for orientation and thus
are highly susceptible to agenda-setting effects.

Political interest, obviously, is closely related to relevance. Thus, high
interest in politics should lead to a high or moderate need for orientation.
The need for orientation, in turn, impacts on an individual's susceptibility to agenda-setting effects.

Second, this result could show the reason that individuals use mass
media in the first place. In other words, this result could indicate the
gratifications sought by respondents. Let's again return to the individuals mentioned in chapter 2. The construction worker, for example, although not normally a high media consumer, may have heard
from a friend about a series that the local newspaper is producing
that deals with crime in the city. Thus, this person may actively seek
out the local newspaper to learn more about this important issue. In
other words, political interest in the issue of crime was the reason the
individual sought out information about the crime issue from the
news media. This individual, in turn, becomes more concerned with
crime as a social problem because of his exposure to crime coverage.
The agenda-setting effect, therefore, would be a natural outcropping
of interest in political issues.

In this case, the motivation was initially generated by an interpersonal
discussion. The conversation activated the political interest of the individual, who sought out additional information for the news media. Thus, the
need for information—or orientation—motivated the individual into using
the news media, which exposed the individual to agenda-setting influences.

Finally, the finding dealing with political interest suggests that
individuals with high motivations let down their guard and thus are
influenced by media messages. Our attorney, a high media user, likely
would also have a high interest in political issues. Because of her high
interest in politics, she likely would not put up defenses to fend off
agenda-setting influences. She would be unlikely to be concerned that
the mass media are manipulating public opinion by creating and over-
emphasizing the media's own political agenda. Thus, the coverage would
influence her without any conscious or subconscious attempt to combat
these influences. Therefore, individuals' need for information outweighs
their concern for manipulation of public opinion by the mass media.
They may not agree with the coverage in the news media, but they
consume it—and are influenced by it—because they have a strong need
for the information contained in their coverage.

Although agenda setting may not be inadvertent, it may be an inevitable
outcome of active information processing. Those most able to put up defense
mechanisms to avoid the news media influence—individuals with high
education levels and efficient communication processing systems—are also
the most susceptible to the agenda-setting effects of news coverage.

• Individuals who view the source of the information most positively are most likely to be influenced by the information distributed by this source.

An important factor could be the purpose behind the media coverage,
as perceived by the media consumer. If individuals believe that the news
media are looking out for the public's welfare, they are highly susceptible
to agenda-setting effects. In this case, individuals believe that issues
covered in the media must be important problems in the community.
The news media would not report unimportant issues because they are
ultimately concerned with the public's welfare.

On the other hand, if individuals believe that the mass media are not
looking out for the public's welfare, they must also believe that the media
are manipulating information to serve some other purpose—such as
their own economic welfare. Here, individuals believe that the issues
covered are not important problems in the community because the
media do not care about the public's welfare. Indeed, this seems to be a
logical connection. If people believe the mass media are not looking out
for their welfare, then the issues they are covering must not address the
issues that are really important in the community. Thus, the really
important issues for the community must be issues other than those
covered by the media, who do not care about the community.

INDIVIDUALS AS ACTIVE PROCESSORS

Overall, the research here supports the notion that individuals are
active processors of mass media messages. As researchers in the area of
uses and gratifications would argue, individuals decide how and why
they use the news media. Thus, individuals determine the magnitude
of agenda-setting effects that they display based on their background,
attitudes, and actions.

These results also point to an information activation model of agenda
setting. As utilitarian theories of motivation argue (see McGuire, 1974),
individuals are problem solvers, approaching each situation as an op-
portunity to gain useful information for coping with life's challenges.
Thus, in the case of the agenda-setting function of the media, individuals
are faced with a challenge—deciding what issues are important to
society. To solve this problem, they use the mass media for cues regarding the relative importance of issues. Issue coverage helps individuals
make sense of the problems facing society. Media coverage, then, is the
means that individuals use to reach their desired end—namely, determining what issues are important to their society.

Motivations to solve this problem of determining issue importance
are key to understanding the mental processing involved in agenda

setting. The stronger the motivation—or in other words, the stronger the need for orientation—the more likely an individual is to demonstrate strong agenda-setting effects. Active processors are most susceptible to the agenda-setting effects of the news media.

This is in sharp contrast to previous research that suggests the least attentive and least active individuals are most likely to be influenced by the news media (e.g., McLeod, Becker, & Byrnes, 1974). The findings here show that individuals do not passively accept media messages. Agenda setting is not a variation of the magic bullet theory of media effects. Media messages do not affect all individuals equally and do not affect inattentive individuals as strongly as active processors.

Therefore, individuals actively seek to fulfill information needs by selecting and using the news media. This motivation to fulfill information needs translates into strong agenda-setting influences.

The results here, then, support the knowledge activation model proposed earlier. In general, agenda-setting effects proceed through stages in which different psychological and behavioral characteristics are activated with varying degrees of success with individuals. Attitudinal variables are first activated within individuals based on the individuals' demographic backgrounds. Older, more highly educated individuals tend to hold the news media in a higher regard and are more interested in political information.

A second psychological variable—reliance on the news media—is activated based on other psychological factors. If individuals view the news media in a positive light and if individuals have a high interest in political news, they form a strong reliance on the news media for information.

Individuals next activate behavioral variables based on their reliance on the media. If individuals are highly reliant on the media for information, they expose themselves to media messages often. Finally, behavioral characteristics of individuals activate knowledge about the relative importance of issues. If individuals use the mass media often and discuss issues with others often, they are highly susceptible to agenda-setting effects.

This knowledge activation model offers an optimistic view of how agenda setting functions in our society as a whole. If the news media are ideally providing citizens with a marketplace of ideas, these ideas are reaching individuals most able to do something about them. In other words, the findings here demonstrate that the media are successful in transmitting salience cues regarding the relative importance of individual issues. The media are most successful in transmitting these salience cues to highly educated, highly motivated individuals who are highly interested in politics. These same individuals are also most likely to be in positions to make changes in society to address these issues. Coverage may not mirror the reality of important issues facing our country today.

Yet, the issues that receive coverage are noticed by individuals with the social standing to enact solutions to these problems.

Although the findings here support the knowledge activation model, there is only limited support for a simple message transferal model of agenda setting. Exposure to media messages correlate with agenda-setting effects. As chapter 4 detailed, if respondents were high media users, they were also highly concerned with the issues covered in the media.

Indeed, exposure to the mass media seems to be crucial for agenda-setting influences to occur. Without some level of exposure to the mass media, individuals must rely on secondary information—through interpersonal communication channels, personal experience, or real-world cues—to acquire information about the relative importance of issues. These secondary sources of information are less efficient than the mass media in transmitting salience cues.

Factors other than media exposure, however, were more critical in the agenda-setting process. Exposure to the mass media was just one factor that influenced individuals' susceptibility to agenda-setting effects. This was especially evident in the full model of agenda setting shown in chapter 5. When other factors, such as education and political interest, were accounted for, exposure to the media did not significantly add to the prediction of agenda-setting susceptibility. Exposure to the mass media, then, was relatively inconsequential in the agenda-setting process. Media exposure, therefore, appears to serve more as a catalyst function in the agenda-setting process. Media exposure activates other factors that have an influence on the magnitude of agenda-setting effects.

Mere exposure to the media does not directly affect agenda-setting influences. Rather, media exposure may heighten psychological variables, such as interest in politics, which, in turn, makes the individual more susceptible to agenda-setting influences. Thus, media exposure activates latent motivations that directly impact on agenda-setting influences.

IMPLICATIONS

Overall, the findings show a link between media effects on the one hand and uses and gratifications on the other. Several points should be made. First, this study does not answer the question of whether mass media audiences are active or passive, an area that Levy and Windahl (1985) called "one of the longest-lived controversies" (p. 109). This study was not concerned with whether the respondents were active or passive, but rather if active respondents differed from passive respondents in the magnitude of agenda-setting effects that they displayed. These findings show differences in the strength of agenda-setting effects between active and passive processors. The results, then, show only that active processing is important in the agenda-setting process—not whether media consumers are active or passive. In general, the more active an individual is, the more powerful the agenda-setting effects they display.

Second, the results do not link agenda setting with participation in the political process. Whereas active individuals are most likely to show agenda-setting effects, this is not to assume that active information seeking leads to active participation in politics. Indeed, Lazarsfeld and Merton (1948), nearly an half century ago, argued that exposure to information in the mass media may "narcotize" rather than energize members of the public. News consumers may substitute knowing about problems facing our country today with doing something about the problems. As Becker (1977) noted, if media consumers would rather read or view action than take action themselves, the news media would have a dysfunctional effect on individuals by insulating them from action.

The results here may provide us with information about the political process in the United States. Low voter turnout has been a concern of political communication scholars for several years. Perhaps we have such low involvement in political process because members of the public are substituting the seeking of information for the action of solving the problems. A key, then, to increasing citizen participation in the political process is to find ways to stimulate the public into actively seeking out political information and putting their newly gained knowledge to work in developing solutions to the problems facing society today.

Although obtaining information may have some negative consequences, these findings also indicate positive aspects of this process. The stronger the motivation to seek information, the more active individuals become. The more active the individual, the better able she or he is to understand the significance of issue coverage in the mass media. Thus, the first stage of public opinion, awareness of a problem, is best undertaken by active participants. Subsequent stages—attitudes about the problems and behavior toward enacting solutions to combat the problem—could be better served by greater involvement by citizens.

FUTURE DIRECTIONS
IN AGENDA-SETTING RESEARCH

Such findings offer several suggestions for future research. First, future research should consider further applications of the agenda-setting susceptibility measure used here. The index has proved to be useful in this book. It has also proved to be useful in examining the role of the gatekeeper in the agenda-setting process (Wanta & Newman, 1996). Researchers may consider applying this measure in new areas with new variables. Indeed, the index is a more accurate measure of the agenda-setting effect.

Second, given the finding that education influenced agenda-setting susceptibility, future research might try to examine more closely potential links between agenda-setting and knowledge gap research. The knowledge gap hypothesis proposes a pessimistic view of media effects. Information in the mass media is helping to create an ever-widening gap in our society between the knowledge rich and the knowledge poor. Are similar implications in store in agenda setting? Is there some sort of an ever-widening gap on issue awareness between the knowledge rich and knowledge poor? Will the knowledge rich always know more about important issues than the knowledge poor? What effects will this issue awareness gap have on society?

Next, if the underlying mental processing of media messages in these two disciplines is somehow theoretically linked, factors that affect the knowledge gap may also influence agenda setting. Thus, future research should examine these knowledge gap variables in an agenda-setting framework. Viswanath and Finnegan (1991), for example, listed 13 factors that have been found to influence the knowledge gap hypothesis. Some of them—such as level of publicity and methodological considerations—have been found to influence the agenda-setting hypothesis as well. Others, however—such as the level of social conflict and the nature of the topic—seem especially applicable to agenda setting. If these variables affect the differential learning abilities of individuals, as previous knowledge gap research suggests, then these same variables may play a role in the social learning of issues salience addressed in agenda-setting research.

In addition, more attention should be devoted to attitudinal variables. Examined here were just four psychological variables: political interest, the two credibility indexes, and reliance, which was examined only in one of the secondary analyses. Yet, it is evident from the results here that attitudes of individuals are critical variables in agenda setting. Other attitudinal variables, such as the uses and gratification measures, should be employed in the future.

Certainly, individuals who use the media "to keep up with the main issues of the day" should differ from individuals who use the media "to be entertained." Individuals motivated to keep up with important issues display stronger susceptibility to agenda-setting effects than individuals motivated to be entertained—if the knowledge activation model of agenda setting is true. Cognitive needs, such as obtaining knowledge about important issues, should strongly influence the agenda-setting process more than affective needs, such as gaining an emotional release from the real world.

Neuman, Just, and Crigler (1992) also noted the importance that motivational variables play in media usage patterns. They concluded that the motivations underlying media usage is more important than the types of coverage that individuals expose themselves to. Thus, they argued that message variables are less significant than the psychological variables possessed by media consumers, a conclusion supported by the results here.

Closely tied to the motivations of individuals is the concept of the need for orientation. It is apparent from the findings here that individuals with a strong political interest were searching for a cognitive map of their environment, striving to map their world. This need for orientation has important implications for social scientists. Both Westley and Barrow (1959) and McCombs (1967) found that editorial endorsements had a more powerful influence on newspaper readers if the readers had a high need for orientation. Clearly, the influence of an individual's need for orientation has the potential to go far beyond the agenda-setting process.

Thus, the motivations of individuals deserve further investigation. By understanding the motivations of individuals, a more focused picture of the agenda-setting process may emerge. It is an area that appears fruitful for future research.

This text also marks a starting point for an expansion of the agenda-setting hypothesis into the largely uncharted area of issue diversity within individuals. Further attention is needed to this area and other possible consequences of the public agenda. Researchers, for instance, should consider other variables that may influence the number of issues with which individuals voice concern.

Agenda diversity, indeed, appears to bear closer scrutiny in the future, given the incredible proliferation of new channels of information now available through the internet, cable television, and satellite broadcast systems. With so many potential sources for issue information, the news media's role in the agenda-setting process may diminish.

Finally, there is still much work to be done in examining individual variables in the agenda-setting process. As this book outlined, agenda-setting effects are not consistent across all individuals. Future research should examine additional variables at the individual level. Through rigorous examinations, a clearer picture will emerge, detailing how individuals process salience cues transmitted by the media.

REFERENCES

Allen, R. L., & Izcaray, F. (1988). Nominal agenda diversity in a media–rich, less–developed society. *Communication Research, 15,* 29–50.

Anderson, J. R., & Bower, G. (1973). *Human associative memory.* Washington, DC: Winston.

Atwater, T., & Fico, F. (1986). Source reliance and use in reporting state government: A study of print and broadcast practices. *Newspaper Research Journal, 8,* 53–61.

Atwater, T., Salwen, M. B., & Anderson, R. B. (1985). Interpersonal discussion as a potential barrier to agenda-setting. *Newspaper Research Journal, 6,* 37–43.

Atwood, L. E., Sohn, A. B., & Sohn, H. (1978). Daily newspaper contributions to community discussion. *Journalism Quarterly, 55,* 570–576.

Ball-Rokeach, S. J., Rokeach, M., & Grube, J. W. (1984). *The great American values test: Influencing behavior and belief through television.* New York: The Free Press.

Becker, L. B. (1979). Measurement of gratifications. *Communication Research, 6,* 54–73.

Becker, L. B., & McCombs, M. E. (1977). *U.S. primary politics and public opinion: The role of the press in determining voter reactions.* Paper presented to the International Communication Association Annual Conference, Berlin, West Germany.

Becker, L. B, Sobowale, I. A., & Cobbey, R. E. (1979). Reporters and their professional and organizational commitment. *Journalism Quarterly, 56,* 753–763.

Becker, L. B., & Whitney, D. C. (1980). Effects of media dependencies. *Communication Research, 7,* 95–120.

Becker, L. E. (1977). The impact of issue saliences. In D. L. Shaw & M. E. McCombs (Eds.), *The emergence of American political issues: The agenda-setting function of the press*(pp. 121–131). St. Paul, MN: West Publishing.

Blumler, J. G., & Katz, E. (1974). *The uses of mass communication: Current perspectives on gratifications research.* Beverly Hills, CA: Sage.

Breed, W. (1955). Newspaper opinion leaders and the process of standardization. *Journalism Quarterly, 32,* 277–284, 328.

Brosius, H., & Kepplinger, H. M. (1992). Linear and nonlinear models of agenda-setting in television. *Journal of Broadcasting & Electronic Media, 36,* 5–23.

Carter, R. F., Stamm, K. R., & Heintz-Knowles, K. (1992). Agenda-setting and consequentiality. *Journalism Quarterly, 69,* 868–877.

Chaffee, S. H. (1972, August). *Longitudinal designs for communication research: Cross-lagged correlations.* Paper presented to the Association for Education in Journalism annual conference, Carbondale, IL.

Chaffee, S. H. (1982). Mass media and interpersonal channels: Competitive, convergent or complementary? In G. Gumpert & R. Cathcart (Eds.), *Intermedia: Interpersonal communication in a media world* (pp. 62–80). New York: Oxford Univeristy Press.

Chaffee, S. H., & Wilson, D. G. (1977). Media rich, media poor: Two studies of diversity in agenda-holding. *Journalism Quarterly, 54,* 466–476.

Cohen, B. C. (1963). *The press and foreign policy.* Princeton, NJ: Princeton University Press.

Coleman, J. S. (1957). *Community conflict.* New York: The Free Press.

Cranberg, G., & Rodriguez, R. (1994). The myth of the minority reader. *Columbia Journalism Review, 32,* 42.

Crouse, T. (1972). *The boys on the bus.* New York: Random House.

Culbertson, H. (1974). Words vs. pictures: Perceived impact and connotative meaning. *Journalism Quarterly, 51,* 226–237.

DeFleur, M. L., & Ball-Rokeach, S. (1989). *Theories of mass communication* (5th ed.). New York: Longman.

Dewey, J. (1922). *Human nature and conduct.* New York: Holt, Rinehart & Winston.

Dewey, J. (1927). *The public and its problems.* New York: Holt, Rinehart & Winston.

Duncan, O., Featherman, D., & Duncan, B. (1972). *Socioeconomic background and achievement.* New York: Seminar Press.

Eaton, H. (1989). Agenda-setting with bi-weekly data on content of three national media. *Journalism Quarterly, 66,* 942–948, 959.

Ebbinghaus, H. (1885). *Uber das Gedachtnis [About memory].* Leipzig: Dunker and Humblot.

Edelstein, A. S. (1993). Thinking about the criterion variable in agenda setting research. *Journal of Communication, 43,* 85–99.

Edelstein, A. S., & Tefft, D. (1974). Media credibility and respondent credulity with respect to Watergate. *Communication Research, 1,* 426–439.

Erbring, L., Goldenberg, E. N., & Miller, A. H. (1980). Front-page news and real-world cues: A new look at agenda-setting by the media. *American Journal of Political Science, 24,* 16–49.

Ferguson, M. A. (1984, May). *Issue diversity and media: Nominal, attributive and field diversity as correlates of media exposure and diversity.* Paper presented at the Annual Convention of the International Communication Association, San Francisco, CA.

Fielder, V. D., & Tipton, L. P. (1986). *Minorities and newspapers.* Washington, DC: American Society of Newspaper Editors.

Funkhouser, G. R. (1973). The issues of the sixties: An exploratory study in the dynamics of public opinion. *Public Opinion Quarterly, 37,* 62–75.

Gaziano, C., & McGrath, K. (1986). Measuring the concept of credibility. *Journalism Quarterly, 63,* 451–462.

Hart, R. P. (1987). *The sound of leadership: Presidential communication in the modern age.* Chicago: The University of Chicago Press.

Hill, D. B. (1985). Viewer characteristics and agenda setting by television news. *Public Opinion Quarterly, 49,* 340–350.

Hirsch, P. (1980). The 'scary world' of the nonviewer and other anomalies: A reanalysis of Gerbner et al.'s findings on cultivation analysis. *Communication Research, 7,* 403–456.

Hong, K., & Shemer, S. (1976, August). *Influence of media and interpersonal agendas on personal agendas.* Paper presented to the Association for Education in Journalism and Mass Communication Annual Convention, Madison, WI.

Hovland, C., Janis, I. L., & Kelley, H. H. (1953). *Communication and persuasion: Psychological studies of opinion change.* New Haven, CT: Yale University Press.

Iyengar, S., & Kinder, D. R. (1987). *News that matters: Television and American opinion.* Chicago: University of Chicago Press.

Iyengar, S., Peters, M. D., & Kinder, D. R. (1982). Experimental Demonstrations of the 'not-so-minimal' consequences of television news programs. *American Political Science Review, 76,* 848–858.

Iyengar, S., Peters, M. D., Kinder, D. R., & Krosnick, J. A. (1984). The evening news and presidential evaluations. *Journal of Personality and Social Psychology, 46,* 778–787.

Jacobs, L. R. & Shapiro, R. Y. (1994). Issues, candidate image, and priming: The use of private polls in Kennedy's 1960 presidential campaign. *American Political Science Review, 88,* 527–540.

Kaheman, D., Slovic, P., & Tversky, A. (1982). *Judgment under uncertainty: Heuristics and biases.* New York: Cambridge University Press.

Katz, E., Blumler, J. G., & Gurevitch, M. (1974). Utilization of mass communication by the individual. In J. G. Blumler & E. Katz (Eds.), *The uses of mass communication: Current perspectives on gratifications research* (pp. 19–32). Beverly Hills, CA: Sage.

Katz, E., & Lazarsfeld, P. F. (1955). *Personal influence.* New York: The Free Press.

Kerlinger, F. N. (1986). *Foundations of behavioral research* (3rd ed.). New York: Harcourt Brace Jovanovich.

Kerner, O. (1968). *Report of the National Advisory Commission on Civil Disorders*. New York: Bantam.

Kinder, D., & Sears, D. O. (1985). Public opinion and political action. In G. Lindzey & E. Aronson (Eds.), *Handbook of social psychology* (pp. 659–741). Reading, MA: Addison–Wesley.

Krosnick, J. A., & Kinder, D. R. (1990). Altering the foundations of support for the president through priming. *American Political Science Review, 84*, 499.

Krugman, H. E. (1965). The impact of television advertising: Learning without involvement. *Public Opinion Quarterly, 29*, 349–356.

Krugman, H. E. (1966). The measurement of advertising involvement. *Public Opinion Quarterly, 30*, 583–596.

Krugman, H. E., & Hartley, E. L. (1970). Passive learning from television. *Public Opinion Quarterly, 34*, 184–190.

Lang, K., & Lang, G. E. (1983). *The battle for public opinion: The president, the press and the polls during Watergate*. New York: Columbia University Press.

Lasorsa, D. L., & Wanta, W. (1990). Effects of personal, interpersonal and media experiences on issue salience. *Journalism Quarterly, 67*, 804–813.

Lazarsfeld, P. F., Berelson, B., & Gaudet, H. (1948). *The people's choice*. New York: Columbia University Press.

Lazarsfeld, P. F., & Merton, R. K. (1948). Mass communication, popular taste and organized social action. In L. Bryson (Ed.), *The communication of ideas* (pp. 95–118). New York: Harper and Brothers.

Lester, P. (1995). *Visual communication: Images with message*. Belmont, CA: Wadsworth.

Levy, M. R., & Windahl, S. (1985). The concept of audience activity. In K. E. Rosengren, L. A. Wenner, & P. Palmgreen (Eds.), *Media gratifications research* (pp. 109–122). Beverly Hills, CA: Sage.

Lowery, S. A. & DeFleur, M. L. (1988). *Milestones in mass communication research* (2nd ed.). New York: Longman.

MacKuen, M. B., & Coombs, S. L. (1981). *More than news: Media power in public affairs*. Beverly Hills, CA: Sage.

Martin, H. J. (1994, August). *How news magazines frame coverage when presidents want to tax and spend*. Paper presented at the Association for Education in Journalism and Mass Communication Annual Convention, Atlanta, GA.

McClure, R. D., & Patterson, T. E. (1976). Print vs. network news. *Journal of Communication, 26*, 23–28.

McCombs, M. E. (1967). Editorial endorsements: A study of influence. *Journalism Quarterly, 44*, 545–548.

McCombs, M. E. (1977). Newspaper versus television: Mass communication effects across times. In D. L. Shaw & M. E. McCombs (Eds.), *The emergence of American political issues: The agenda-setting function of the press* (pp. 89–105). St. Paul, MN: West Publishing.

McCombs, M. E. (1981). The agenda-setting approach. In D. D. Nimmo & K. R. Sanders (Eds.), *Handbook of political communication* (pp. 121–140). Beverly Hills, CA: Sage.

McCombs, M. E. (1992). Explorers and surveyors: Expanding strategies for agenda-setting research. *Journalism Quarterly, 69*, 813–824.

McCombs, M. E., Danielian, L., & Wanta, W. (1995). Issues in the news and the public agenda: The agenda-setting tradition. In T. L. Glasser & C. T. Salmon (Eds.), *Public opinion and the communication of consent* (pp. 281–300). New York: Guilford.

McCombs, M. E., & Poindexter, P. (1983). The duty to keep informed: News exposure and civic obligation. *Journal of Communication, 33*, 88–96.

McCombs, M. E., & Shaw, D. L. (1972). The agenda-setting function of mass media. *Public Opinion Quarterly, 36*, 176–187.

McCombs, M. E., & Weaver, D. H. (1985). Toward a merger of gratifications and agenda-setting research. In K. E. Rosengren, L. A. Wenner, & P. Palmgreen. (Eds.), *Media gratifications research* (pp. 95–108). Beverly Hills, CA: Sage.

McCombs, M. E., & Zhu, J. H. (1994, July). *Diversity, volatility and paradigm shift in the public issue agenda from 1939 to 1993.* Paper presented at the Annual Convention of the International Communication Association, Sydney, Australia.

McDonald, D. G. (1990). Media orientation and television news viewing. *Journalism Quarterly, 67,* 11–20.

McGuire, W. J. (1974). Psychological motives and communication gratifications. In J. G. Blumler & E. Katz (Eds.), *The uses of mass communication: Current perspectives on gratifications research*(pp. 167–196). Beverly Hills, CA: Sage.

McLeod, J. M., Becker, L. B., & Byrnes, J. E. (1974). Another look at the agenda-setting function of the press. *Communication Research, 1,* 131–166.

McLeod, J. M., & McDonald, D. G. (1985). Beyond simple exposure: Media orientations and their impact on political processes. *Communication Research, 12,* 3–33.

McLuhan, M. (1964). Understanding media: The extensions of man. New York: McGraw-Hill.

McManus, J. H. (1994). Market-driven journalism: Let the citizen beware? Thousand Oaks, CA: Sage.

McNamara, T. P. (1992). Theories of priming: I. associative distance and lag. *Journal of Experimental Psychology: Learning, Memory, and Cognition, 18,* 1173–1190.

Meadowcroft, J. M., & Olson, B. (1995, August). *Television viewing vs. reading: Testing information processing assumptions.* Paper presented at the annual meeting of the Association for Education in Journalism and Mass Communication, Washington, DC.

Mendelsohn, M. (1994). The media's persuasive effects: The priming of leadership in the 1988 Canadian election. *Canadian Journal of Political Science, 27,* 81–97.

Meyer, P. (1989). Defining and measuring credibility of newspapers: Developing an index. *Journalism Quarterly, 66,* 567–574, 588.

Mullins, L. E. (1973). *Agenda-setting on the campus: The mass media and learning of issue importance in the '72 election.* Paper presented to the Association for Education in Journalism and Mass Communication annual Convention, Fort Collins, CO.

Mullins, L. E. (1977). Agenda-setting and the young voter. In D. L. Shaw & M. E. McCombs (Eds.), *The emergence of American political issues: The agenda-setting function of the press* (pp. 133–148). St. Paul, MN: West Publishing.

Neuman, W. R., Just, M. R., & Crigler, A. N. (1992). *Common knowledge: News and the construction of political meaning.* Chicago: University of Chicago Press.

Park, R. E. (1925). Immigrant community and immigrant press. *American Review, 3,* 143–152.

Pedhazur, E. J. (1982). Multiple regression in behavioral research: Explanation and prediction (2nd ed.). New York: Holt, Rinehart & Winston.

Popkin, S. L. (1991). The reasoning voter: Communication and persuasion in presidential campaigns. Chicago: University of Chicago Press.

Price, V., & Tewksbury, D. (1995, July). *News values and public opinion: A theoretical account of media priming and framing.* Paper presented at the Annual Convention of the International Communication Association, Albuquerque, NM.

Protess, D. L., Leff, D. R., Brooks, S. C., & Gordon, M. T. (1985). Uncovering rape: The watchdow press and the limits of agenda-setting. *Public Opinion Quarterly, 49,* 19–37.

Rimmer, T., & Weaver, D. H. (1987). Different questions, different answers? Media use and media credibility. *Journalism Quarterly, 64,* 28–36, 44.

Rogers, E. M., & Shoemaker, F. (1971). *Communication of innovations: A cross-cultural approach.* New York: The Free Press.

Roling, N. G., Ascroft, J., & WaChege, F. (1976). The diffusion of innovations and the issue of equity in rural development. *Communication Research, 3,* 155–169.

Salomon, G. (1979). Interaction of media, cognition and learning. San Francisco: Jossey-Bass.

Salwen, M. B. (1988). Effect of accumulation of coverage on issue salience in agenda-setting. *Journalism Quarterly, 65,* 100–106, 130.

Schoenbach, K. (1982, May). *Agenda-setting effects of print and television in West Germany.* Paper presented at the International Communication Association Annual Convention, Boston, MA.

Schoenbach, K., & Weaver, D. H. (1983, May). *Cognitive bonding and need for orientation during political campaigns.* Paper presented at the International Communication Association Annual Convention, Dallas, TX.

Shaw, D. L., & Clemmer, C. L. (1977). News and the public response. In D. L. Shaw & M. E. McCombs (Eds.) *The emergence of American political issues: The agenda-setting function of the press* (pp. 33–51). St. Paul, MN: West Publishing.

Shaw, D. L., & McCombs, M. E. (1977). *The emergence of American political issues: The agenda-setting function of the press.* St. Paul, MN: West Publishing.

Singer, J. L. (1980). The power and limitations of television: A cognitive-affective analysis. In P. H. Tannenbaum (Ed.), *The entertainment functions of television* (pp. 31–65). Hillsdale, NJ: Lawrence Erlbaum Associates.

Singletary, M. (1976). Components of credibility of a favorable news source. *Journalism Quarterly, 53,* 316–319

Sohn, A. B. (1978). A longitudinal analysis of local non-political agenda-setting effects. *Journalism Quarterly, 55,* 325–333.

Son, J., Reese, S. D., & Davie, W. R. (1987). Effects of visual–verbal redundancy and recaps on television news learning. *Journal of Broadcasting & Electronic Media, 31,* 207–216.

Stone, G. C. (1987). *Examining newspapers: What research reveals about America's newspapers.* Beverly Hills, CA: Sage.

Stone, G. C., & McCombs, M. E. (1981). Tracing the time lag in agenda-setting. *Journalism Quarterly, 58,* 51–55.

Tichenor, P., Donohue, G., & Olien, C. (1970). Mass media flow and differential growth in knowledge. *Public Opinion Quarterly, 34,* 159–170.

Tipton, L., Haney, R. D., & Baseheart, J. R. (1975). Media agenda-setting in city and state election campaigns. *Journalism Quarterly, 52,* 15–22.

Viswanath, K., & Finnegan, J., Jr. (1991, May). *The knowledge gap hypothesis: Twenty years later.* Paper presented at the Annual Convention of the Internatioanl Communication Association, Chicago, IL.

Wanta, W. (1991). Presidential approval ratings as a variable in the agenda-building process. *Journalism Quarterly, 68,* 672–679.

Wanta, W., & Foote, J. (1994). The president–news media relationship: A time series analysis of agenda-setting. *Journal of Broadcasting & Electronic Media, 38,* 437–448.

Wanta, W., & Newman, J. (1996, May). *Newspaper editors and the national agenda: The role of the gatekeepers in the agenda-setting process.* Paper presented to the International Communication Association Annual Convention, Chicago, IL.

Wanta, W., Stephenson, M. A., Turk, J., & McCombs, M. E. (1989). How president's state of union talk influenced news media agenda. *Journalism Quarterly, 66,* 537–541.

Wanta, W., & Wu, Y. C. (1992). Interpersonal communication and the agenda-setting process. *Journalism Quarterly, 69,* 847–855

Watt, J. H., Mazza, M., & Snyder, L. B. (1993). Agenda-setting effects of television news coverage and the memory decay curve. *Communication Research, 20,* 408–435.

Weaver, D. H. (1977). Political issues and voter need for orientation. In D. L. Shaw & M. E. McCombs (Eds.), *The emergence of American political issues: The agenda-setting function of the press* (pp. 107–120). St. Paul, MN: West Publishing.

Weaver, D. H. (1984). Media agenda-setting and public opinion: Is there a link? In R. N. Bostrom & B. H. Westley (Eds.), *Communication yearbook 8* (pp. 680–691). Beverly Hills, CA: Sage.

Weaver, D. H., Auh, T. S., Stehla, T. A., & Wilhoit, G. C. (1975, August). *A path analysis of individual agenda-setting during the 1974 Indiana senatorial campaign.* Paper presented to the Association for Education in Journalism and Mass Communication Annual Convention, Ottawa, Canada.

Weaver, D. H., Graber, D. A., McCombs, M. E., & Eyal, C. H. (1981). *Media agenda-setting in a presidential election.* New York: Praeger.

Weaver, D. H., & Mauro, J. B. (1978). Newspaper readership patterns. *Journalism Quarterly, 55,* 84–91, 134

Weimann, G. (1994). *The influentials: People who influence people.* Albany, NY: SUNY Press.

Westley, B. H., & Barrow, L. (1959). An investigation of news seeking behavior. *Journalism Quarterly, 36,* 431–438.

Winter, J. P. (1981). Contingent conditions in the agenda-setting process. In G. C. Wilhoit & H. deBock (Eds.), *Mass communication review yearbook* (Vol. 2, pp. 235–243). Beverly Hills, CA: Sage.

Winter, J. P., & Eyal, C. (1981). Agenda-setting for the civil rights issue. *Public Opinion Quarterly, 45,* 376–383.

Woodworth, R. S., & Schlosberg, H. (1954). *Experimental psychology* (rev. ed.). New York: Henry Holt & Company.

Zhu, J. H. (1992). Issue competition and attention distraction: A zero-sum theory of agenda-setting. *Journalism Quarterly, 69,* 825–836.

Zucker, H. G. (1978). The variable nature of news media influence. In B. D. Ruben (Ed.), *Communication yearbook 2* (pp. 225–240). New Brunswick, NJ: Transaction.

Author Index

A

Allen, R. L., 93, 111
Anderson, J. R., 85, 111
Anderson, R. B., 3, 8, 111
Ascroft, J., 39, 111
Atwater, T., 3, 8, 3, 38, 111
Atwood, L. E., 14, 40, 111
Auh, T. S., 36, 111

B

Ball-Rokeach, S. J., 57, 58, 111
Barrow, L., 110, 116
Baseheart, J. R., 14, 70, 77, 115
Becker, L. B., 10, 58, 70, 92, 95, 106, 108, 111, 114
Berelson, B., 41, 113
Blumler, J. G., 5, 6, 111, 112
Bower, G., 85, 111
Breed, W., 71, 111
Brooks, S. C., 11, 114
Brosius, H., 12, 111
Byrnes, J. E., 10, 106, 114

C

Carter, R. F., 100, 111
Chaffee, S. H., 39, 69, 93, 94, 99, 111
Clemmer, C. L., 115
Cobbey, R. E., 58, 111
Cohen, B. C., 34, 111
Coleman, J. S., 39, 111
Coombs, S. L., 11, 26, 40, 113
Cranberg, G., 21, 111
Crigler, A. N., 109, 114

Crouse, T., 71, 111
Culbertson, H., 66, 111

D

Danielian, L., 9, 113
Davie, W. R., 66, 115
DeFleur, M. L., 57, 58, 74, 111, 113
Dewey, J., 20, 111, 112
Donohue, G., 102, 115
Duncan, B., 20, 112
Duncan, O., 20, 112

E

Eaton, H., 70, 112
Ebbinghaus, H., 71, 72, 112
Edelstein, A. S., 39, 100, 112
Erbring, L., 3, 12, 26, 36, 38, 40, 58, 112
Eyal, C., 116
Eyal, C. H., 3, 11, 14, 69, 70, 116

F

Featherman, D., 20, 112
Ferguson, M. A., 93, 112
Fico, F., 111
Fielder, V. D., 21, 22, 112
Finnegan, J., Jr., 109, 115
Foote, J., 14, 115
Funkhouser, G. R., 9, 10, 70, 112

G

Gaudet, H., 41, 113
Gaziano, C., 28, 112

117

Goldenberg, E. N., 3, 112
Gordon, M. T. , 11, 114
Graber, D. A., 3, 116
Grube, J. W., 58, 111
Gurevitch, M., 6, 112

H

Haney, R. D., 14, 70, 77, 115
Hart, R. P., 80, 112
Hartley, E. L., 65, 113
Heintz-Knowles, K., 100, 111
Hill, D. B., 3, 16, 21, 22, 94, 100, 112
Hirsch, P., 17, 112
Hong, K., 3, 36, 38, 112
Hovland, C., 25, 28, 112
Hu, Y.W., 90, 100

I

Iyengar, S., 11, 12, 27, 79, 86, 112
Izcaray, F., 93, 111

J

Jacobs, L. R., 86, 112
Janis, I. L., 25, 112
Just, M. R., 109, 114

K

Kaheman, D., 86, 112
Katz, E., 5, 6, 39, 111, 112
Kelley, H. H., 25, 112
Kepplinger, H. M., 12, 111
Kerlinger, F. N., 20, 112
Kerner, O., 22, 113
Kinder, D., 113
Kinder, D. R., 11, 12, 26, 27, 79, 86, 112, 113
Krosnick J. A., 86, 112, 113
Krugman, H. E., 64, 65, 113

L

Lang, G. E., 11, 113
Lang, K., 11, 113
Lasorsa, D. L., 12, 16, 18, 36, 38, 40, 113
Lazarsfeld, P. F., 39, 41, 108, 112, 113
Leff, D. R., 11, 114
Lester, P., 66, 113
Levy, M. R., 107, 113
Lowery, S. A., 74, 113

M

MacKuen, M. B., 11, 26, 40, 113
Martin, H. J., 80, 113
Mauro, J. B., 22, 116
Mazza, M., 72, 115
McClure, R. D., 40, 68, 70, 77, 113
McCombs, M. E., 1, 2, 3, 5, 7, 8, 9, 10, 25, 27, 28, 33, 39, 40, 42, 45, 47, 68, 69, 70, 77, 80, 86, 93, 96, 100, 101, 110, 111, 113, 114, 115, 116
McDonald, D. G., 58, 114
McGrath, K., 28, 112
McGuire, W. J., 3, 47, 105, 114
McLeod, J. M., 10, 26, 36, 38, 40, 58, 106, 114
McLuhan, M., 62, 63, 114
McManus, J. H., 25, 114
McNamara, T. P., 85, 114
Meadowcraft, J. M., 114
Mendelsohn, M., 86, 114
Merton, R. K., 108, 113
Meyer, P., 29, 31, 114
Miller, A. H., 3, 112
Miller, R., 90
Mullins, L. E., 26, 36, 38, 41, 70, 114

N

Neuman, W. R., 109, 114
Newman, J., 108, 115

O

Olien, C., 102, 115
Olson, B., 114

P

Palmgreen, P., 28
Park, R. E., 20, 114
Patterson, T. E., 40, 68, 70, 77, 113
Pedhazur, E. J., 50, 114
Peters, M. D., 27, 86, 112
Poindexter, P., 25, 96, 113
Popkin, S. L., 95, 114
Price, V., 19, 87, 114
Protess, D. L., 11, 114

R

Reese, S. D., 66, 115
Rimmer, T., 28, 34, 114
Rodriguez, R., 21, 111

Rogers, E. M., 41, 44, 114
Rokeach, M., 58, 111
Roling, N. G., 39, 114
Rosengren, K. E., 28

S

Salomon, G., 65, 115
Salwen, M. B., 3, 8, 69, 70, 111, 115
Schleuder, J., 86
Schlosberg, H., 71, 73, 116
Schoenbach, K., 11, 115
Sears, D. O., 26, 113
Shapiro, R. Y., 86, 112
Shaw, D. L., 1, 2, 3, 7, 8, 9, 10, 39, 42, 45, 70, 77, 79, 93, 100, 101, 113, 115
Shemer, S., 3, 36, 38, 112
Shoemaker, F., 41, 44, 114
Singer, J. L., 63, 64, 115
Singletary, M., 28, 115
Slovic, P., 86, 112
Snyder, L. B., 72, 115
Sobowale, I. A., 58, 111
Sohn, A. B., 14, 70, 111, 115
Sohn, H., 14, 111
Son, J., 66, 115
Stamm, K. R., 100, 111
Stehla, T. A., 36, 116
Stephenson, M. A., 3, 80, 115
Stone, G. C., 21, 25, 54, 69, 70, 92, 94, 115

T

Tefft, D., 39, 112
Tewksbury, D., 19, 87, 114

Tichenor, P., 102, 115
Tipton, L., 14, 70, 77, 115
Tipton, L. P., 14, 21, 22, 70, 77, 112
Turk, J. V., 3, 80, 115
Tversky, A., 86, 112

V

Viswanath, K., 109, 115

W

WaChege, F., 39, 115
Wanta, W., 3, 4, 9, 12, 14, 16, 18, 36, 38, 40, 44, 80, 86, 90, 100, 108, 113, 115
Watt, J. H., 72, 115
Weaver, D. H., 2, 3, 5, 9, 10, 11, 12, 17, 22, 26, 27, 28, 32, 34, 36, 38, 47, 57, 58, 114, 115, 116
Weimann, G., 33, 39, 116
Wenner, L. A., 28
Westley, B. H., 110, 116
Whitney, D. C., 58, 111
Wilhoit, G. C., 36, 116
Wilson, D. G., 93, 94, 99, 111
Windahl, S., 107, 113
Winter, J. P. , 11, 14, 26, 36, 38, 69, 70, 116
Woodworth, R. S., 71, 73, 116
Wu, Y. C., 36, 38, 44, 115

Z

Zhu, J. H., 70, 93, 100, 114, 116
Zucker, H. G., 14, 69, 70, 100, 116

Subject Index

A

ABC World News Tonight, 14, 73
Adverting information, 95–100
Agenda diversity,
  see Issue diversity
Agenda-setting susceptibility measure, 1–2,
    13–19, 32–35, 37, 41–47, 49–56, 58,
    108–109
Aggregate data, 7, 8, 9, 11–12, 74
Automaton studies, 10–12, 17

B

Behavioral variables, 4, 18, 36–45, 48–50,
    52–56, 60, 101

C

Civic duty, 96–99
Cognition, 2, 3, 49, 63, 86
Cognitive portrait studies, 11
Crime issue, 13, 14, 16, 38
Cultivation theory, 17

D

Demographics, 3, 18–19, 20–24, 48–57, 59–60,
    92–99, 101–103, 106
  Age, 20–24, 51–56, 59–60, 92, 94, 97–99
  Education, 20–24, 48, 51–57, 59–60, 92,
    94–97, 101–103, 106
  Gender, 20–24, 51–52, 54, 96–97
  Income, 20–24, 48, 51–52, 54–55, 92, 94,
    96–97
  Race, 20–24, 51–52, 54

E

Economic issues, 6–7, 12, 13, 14, 16, 79
Election campaigns, 10
Emnid, 12
Environment/pollution issue, 8, 13, 14, 16
Eugene register-guard, 14
Experiments, 11–12, 86

G

Gestalt, 63

I

Images of candidates, 3
Information processing, 6, 7, 19, 26, 36, 43,
    48–49, 53–54, 62, 64–65, 76, 101,
    105, 108
International problems issue, 14–16, 38, 75, 79
Interpersonal communication, 3, 4, 17, 36–40,
    41–49, 51–53, 55, 60, 107
  Types of discussion, 45–47
  Role in discussions, 45–47
Involvement, 63–64
Issue awareness, 7
Issue diversity, 92–100, 110
Issue salience, 2–3, 6, 17–18, 20, 86

K

Knowledge activation, 18–19, 87–91, 106–107
Knowledge gap, 102–103, 109

M

Mass persuasion studies, 9–10, 12
Media conformity index, 12

121

Media dependency theory, 57
Media differences, 14, 62–78
Media exposure, 18–19, 22, 27, 36–37, 40–45,
    49, 51–53, 55–56, 59–61, 81–84,
    92–95, 98–99, 107, 109
Memory, 19, 63–64
Memory decay, 69, 71–78, 86
Message transferral, 17–18, 44, 107
Most important problem question, 2, 12, 71–72

N

Natural history studies, 11–12
Need for Orientation, 27–28, 57, 103–104, 106,
    110
The New York Times, 11, 71
Newsweek magazine, 10

O

Operationalizing the agenda-setting effect, 7–18

P

Personal experience/obtrusiveness of issues, 17,
    107
Priming, 85–99
Psychological factors, 3, 4, 18–19, 20, 24–35,
    48–61, 85–91, 93–95, 101, 103–106,
    109–110
Political interest, 24–27. 29–33, 48–49,
    51–57, 60, 94, 101, 104, 106

Media credibility, 24–25, 27–34, 51–61,
    101, 105
Media reliance, 57–61
Party affiliation, 34–35
Political philosophy, 34–35
Public officials, 3, 4, 15, 79–91, 101–102
U.S. President, 3, 4, 15, 79–91, 102

S

Schema, 63–64
Single–issue studies, 11–12
Social learning, 2, 7, 20, 57, 65, 101
Sources of the media agenda, 3, 4
Southern Illinoisan, 14
State of the Union address, 15, 79–84, 86–91

T

Tampa Tribune, 14
Time-lag, 14, 69–71, 74–78
Time magazine, 10
Two-step flow, 41

U

Uses and gratifications, 3, 5, 47, 92, 95, 97, 104,
    107, 109
U.S. News & World Report, 10

Z

Zero-Sum game, 70